THE TEACHER AND RELIGION

The EDUCATION and RELIGION Series

Joint Editors: F. H. Hilliard, Ph.D.
and K. N. Kibblewhite, Ph.D.

THE TEACHER AND RELIGION

by

F. H. HILLIARD, Ph.D., B.D.

Senior Lecturer in Religious Education
University of London Institute of Education

JAMES CLARKE & CO LTD
33 STORE STREET
LONDON, WC1

MADE AND PRINTED IN GREAT BRITAIN BY
THE GARDEN CITY PRESS LIMITED
LETCHWORTH, HERTFORDSHIRE

CONTENTS

INTRODUCTION

THE first noteworthy attempt to assess the place which, *on sound educational grounds,* religion could and should have in the curricula and life of what we now call county schools appeared less than twenty-five years ago with the publication of the Spens Report — *Secondary Education, with special reference to Grammar Schools and Technical High Schools.*[1] Its chapter on 'Religious Knowledge' marked the end of a long period, first of controversy on the subject, and later of uneasy silence about it, during which any objective consideration of the place which religion should have in general education would scarcely have been possible. By 1923, however, the first signs of a fresh and promising approach were to be seen. In the West Riding of Yorkshire, and in Cambridgeshire the following year, groups of teachers and representatives of the Churches had come together and produced, with the blessing of the Education Authorities, the first two Agreed Syllabuses of Religious Instruction. These first Agreed Syllabuses were important enough, of course, in themselves as aids to those teachers who sorely needed guidance about how to present religion to children in schools. But they had a greater significance as well. They revealed the emergence of a new approach to the whole question of the place of religion in that part of the education system over which the Churches had no control. The significance of these attempts by teachers and representatives of the Churches to think *educationally* about religion in schools was not lost on the central Authority which quietly

[1] H.M.S.O., 1938.

encouraged them in various ways. The Spens Report, coming fifteen years after the appearance of the first Agreed Syllabus, added its full and authoritative blessing in the shape of a well-reasoned chapter on the principles, aims and methods of the teaching of religious knowledge in the secondary school.

In one sense, then, religious education, as it is now generally called, is a comparative late-comer to the State schools of this country. That it had some place in the teaching and general life of many of these schools long before 1923 is well known but this was largely because some Local Education Authorities, individual Heads and teachers were concerned that this should be so. Thus, a number of Local Authorities made syllabuses of religious teaching available to the schools in their area, and between 1920 and 1930 several handbooks were produced for teachers.[1] In certain Training Colleges, moreover, some good teaching of Divinity was being done. Thus in the early 1930's there were many teachers who were concerned to associate together for the further promotion of good religious education in the schools. In 1930 the Free Churches and kindred bodies such as the Y.M. and Y.W.C.A., set up a Council of Christian Education with a Day School Syllabus Committee. In 1934 was founded the Institute of Christian Education, to bring together for discussion and joint action those who were concerned for the place of religion in education at school, Training College or University.

It is therefore understandable that from 1938 onwards, and more precisely, after 1944, religious education in schools began to acquire educational respectability. Sound educational reasons had been advanced for its having a place in the curriculum and general life of every school and the teaching of religious knowledge had been shown to be perfectly capable of conforming to the kind of principles and methods of teaching which obtained in connection with

---

[1] A noteworthy example was Helen Wodehouse's book, *The Scripture Lesson in the Elementary School*. S.C.M. Press, 1926.

other 'subjects'. It was thus freed from the suspicion of being a back-door by which the evangelising activities of the various Churches could find their way into the State schools.

The significance of this far-reaching change of outlook about the place which religion, and especially teaching about religion, should have in the life of county schools has not always been widely appreciated and understood within the schools themselves. This has been due in some measure to the fact that much too little has been written about it. This in turn has been partly because the less imaginative spirits in the Churches saw it as an attempt to introduce into the schools a 'watered-down version' of Christian teaching instead of the positive advance that in fact it was. At all events, a new generation of teachers is now at work in the schools which understands all too little about these changes of attitude which manifested themselves during the pre-war years. In consequence they have too often been allowed to slip back into earlier and unsatisfactory attitudes towards the place of religion in schools, with all their consequent problems and perplexities. To judge from the kind of comments made and questions asked by younger teachers today at courses and conferences, it is still too commonly assumed that the teaching of religious knowledge in State schools amounts to an extension of Church evangelistic work which could be done sincerely (so it is imagined) only by teachers whose main aim is to 'convert' children to Christianity. The second stage in the argument follows on naturally — that this kind of proselytism is out of place in county schools and therefore religious education ought to be excluded from such schools. This, of course, represents one extreme among the views held by teachers. At the other extreme are to be found teachers who are themselves enthusiastic members of one or other of the Churches, are therefore in favour of giving religious education an important place in the life of the schools, but are in need of some help in the difficult business of working out a sound approach to religious education which reconciles their personal interest with their obligations as teachers working in county schools. Occupying a variety of intermediate positions between these two extremes is a large body of others who have not been able to commit themselves to a whole-hearted acceptance of the Christian religion but who feel that the children have a right to find in it something for themselves if religion can be presented to them in school in a way which does not cut across sound educational principles — principles that is, which require the teacher to teach but preclude him from attempting to convert.

It seems clear then, that a volume is long overdue in which the attempt is made to set out again at some length the *educational* approach to religious education — the principles which give it its *raison d'être*, the aims which are proper to it in a county school setting, the methods by which it can properly be taught, and the outlook and qualifications of the people who teach it. It is with this aim in mind that this book has been written. It also attempts to go on to consider other important practical implications involved in this kind of approach—problems of the use of Agreed Syllabuses, the presentation of religion to younger and older children, the function of a School Assembly, the place of external examinations in religious knowledge, and the contribution which can be made to religious education by the teacher of other subjects. It is written by a teacher for teachers, and for those who intend to become teachers. Its approach throughout is educational but not on that account, it is to be hoped, lacking in sound theology.

It could not have been written at all without the assistance of the teachers and students with whom the author has had the privilege of discussing these matters over a period of eight years and more. From them he has learned a great deal and it is to them that he would wish to dedicate this book, with the hope that they and others like them may possibly find in it some little encouragement to press ahead in this most important part of their work with a renewed sense of its value and its potentialities.

Professor W. R. Niblett, Dean of the University of London Institute of Education, and Dr. K. N. Kibblewhite, Senior Lecturer in Divinity at Southlands College, have been kind enough to look through the MS and have made some valuable suggestions for its correction and improvement. To them the author is especially grateful. He alone, however, must be held responsible for the views set forth.

London,   F.H.H.
1963

CHAPTER 1

RELIGION IN ENGLISH EDUCATION

IT is sometimes assumed that the provisions made in the Education Act of 1944 for Religious Education in schools marked a radical change in the history of English education and educational legislation. This is not so. That there were new elements in this part of the 1944 legislation is true, the most important being, of course, that the provision of religious teaching and of a daily act of worship were made obligatory on all schools. The fact is often lost sight of, however, that the requirements of the 1944 Act with regard to religious education in schools were in line with the spirit and trend of English education as far back as we can trace it, and certainly followed the general direction of earlier legislation. These facts are so germane to the whole approach adopted in this book that no apology is made for inflicting on the reader the historical substantiation of them which follows.

It will be recalled that in England, as in other European countries, such general education as existed from the 7th century onwards was in the hands of the Church, and remained so up to about the period of the Renaissance, that is, till the 15th/16th centuries. During the whole of this time English education knew no divorce between 'religious' and 'secular' education. Whether in monastic or parochial schools, learning and faith together provided the basis as well as the end of all education. Thus the first seven to eight hundred years of English education served among other things to lay the foundations of the conviction, never since lost, that religion is inseparably linked with education.

The influence which the Renaissance began to exert upon English education stemmed from the North European Renaissance movement with its Christian humanism, rather than from the largely a-religious humanism of the Southern Renaissance. Not the least important result of this fact was that in the changes which followed, the new schools which were founded were still inspired by a desire to ensure that the children who were admitted to them should be brought up in the Christian faith and trained in the Christian way of life. A good example of this attitude is found in the statutes of St. Paul's School, founded in 1510 by the famous reformer Dean Colet of St. Paul's with the assistance of Erasmus. While the statutes laid great emphasis on the need for the study of good literature, both Latin and Greek, for its own sake, they also declared that the aim of the school was 'to increase knowledge, and worshipping of God and Our Lord Jesus Christ, and good Christian life and manners in the children'. A similar aim was frequently expressed in the statutes of the grammar schools which were founded or re-founded in the late 16th and early 17th centuries by kings, bishops, country gentlemen, wealthy merchants and city guilds. Thus English education survived the twin upheavals of Renaissance and Reformation with the earlier religious associations changed indeed in outward form — since the Church was no longer in control — but still strong in influence.

Later, in the 18th and 19th centuries, the influence of religion made itself felt in a new and wider field of education when the Church of England and the Free Churches took the initiative in making elementary education available to the poor. The Anglican Society for Promoting Christian Knowledge, which was formed in 1698, had among its aims the foundation of schools to give the children of these people a sound education, religious and secular. By 1754 the Society claimed that by its efforts 2,044 elementary schools had been established, providing education for over 50,000 children. In 1811 this part of the Society's work was taken over by the newly-established National Society for Promoting the Education of the Poor in the Principles of the Established Church. One year earlier the Non-Conformist British and Foreign School Society had come into existence with similar aims but inspired by the desire to spread the Free Church interpretation of the Christian religion. Meantime 'Sunday Schools' had been opened in towns and villages and were providing a very limited education based on Bible reading and the teaching of Christian principles and morality. These schools were the fruits of the work of a number of individuals — Christian philanthropists like Robert Raikes and Hannah More, whose educational aims were undoubtedly very limited and who were not infrequently criticised on that account.[1] The first State grant for Education (£20,000) was made in 1833 and was distributed through the National Society (£11,000) and the British and Foreign School Society (£9,000). The Committee of the Privy Council on Education, which was the State authority on education from 1839 until the creation of the Education Department in 1856, laid it down that 'religion ought to be combined with the whole matter of instruction and regulate the entire system of discipline'.[2]

It will be apparent then, that in this matter of the provision of elementary education for the masses of the poorer people in this country the Churches had taken the initiative and that, in so doing, they had once again asserted, in a new educational field, the conviction that religion is concerned with general education and that general education must embrace religious teaching. When therefore, the Elementary Education Bill was introduced into Parliament in 1870, the

[1] Some of the pioneers of the Sunday School movement actually declared that to make a full education available to the poor would be to run the risk of endangering the whole social structure. See, e.g., the letters of Hannah More (1745–1833) in *English Letters of the XIX Century*, ed. James Aitken, Pelican Books, London, 1946, pp. 49–59.

[2] *History of Education in England*, 1792–1902, J. W. Adamson, Cambridge, 1930, p. 125.

aim of which was described by its author, Mr. W. E. Forster, as being 'To bring elementary education within the reach of every English home', there was no doubt in anybody's mind that religious teaching must be given its proper place in a system which was to be formally approved by the State. The controversy which arose as to the provision of religious education centred, not upon whether or not it should be made: that was taken for granted by nearly everyone. It was concerned with the further question whether religious teaching could be allowed to take on denominational colour in schools to be supported by public funds. Forster himself, during the course of the debate, asserted:

'We have no doubt whatever that an enormous majority of the parents of this country prefer that there should be a Christian training for their children—that they should be taught to read the Bible. If we are to prevent religious teaching altogether, we must say that the Bible shall not be used in schools at all. But would it not be a monstrous thing that the Bible which, after all, is the foundation of the religion we profess, should be the only book that was not allowed to be used in our schools? But then it may be said that we ought to have no dogmatic teaching. But how are we to prevent it? Are we to step in and say that the Bible may be read, but may not be explained? Are we to pick out Bible lessons with the greatest care in order that nothing of a doctrinal character might be taught to the children? . . . I say that is (a question) of detailed supervision which does not belong to the central government.'[1]

In the end, the Elementary Education Act of that year affirmed the principle that non-sectarian religious instruction could be given in schools supported by public funds. It should however, be given at the beginning or end of the school day, so as to allow parents who had conscientious objections to withdraw their children from such instruction with the minimum of interruption to the school time-table.

[1] Verbatim report of debate in Parliament during the progress of the Elementary Education Bill, 1870. National Education Union, London, n.d., p. 14. Note how Forster uses the words 'dogmatic' and 'doctrinal' as though they were synonymous.

It fell to the School Boards which Parliament set up to decide whether and what religious instruction should be provided within these limits in the Board schools in their area. Many of the Boards followed the lead given by the London Board which declared that:

> 'The Bible shall be read, and there shall be given such explanations and such instruction therefrom in the principles of (the Christian—added 1894) religion and of morality as are suited to the capacities of children.'[1]

Thus what Professor Trevelyan has called 'the Bible religion of the English'[2] became an accepted part of the new State elementary education system and found a place similarly in the curricula of the new State secondary schools which developed as a result of the Education Act of 1902.

Unfortunately, the task of the School Boards and the teachers who attempted to implement these policies was made extremely difficult by the critical and even hostile attitudes displayed by certain groups within the Churches. Thus in London a bitter wrangle was begun by Mr. Athelstan Riley, an ardent member of the Anglo-Catholic party in the Church of England and a member of the Board. It was alleged that in certain schools teachers were presenting the Bible to children in such a way as to undermine some of the basic doctrines of the Christian religion. So persistently did Mr. Riley and others press these complaints upon the committees of the Board that for a time its business was brought almost to a complete standstill. This kind of controversy tended to make educationists so weary of, and indeed apprehensive about, the possibility of satisfactorily implementing the various provisions made in regard to religious education in schools, that they sometimes did little about it. In practice it was largely left to individual schools and teachers to decide how much religious teaching should be given and how well

---

[1] *London at School, the Story of the School Board.* **H. B. Philpott.** London, 1904, p. 106.

[2] In *English Social History.* London, 1942, p. 552.

it should be done. That some did it well was mainly due to their own enthusiasm and hard work. The sad fact is that it was not until 1923, when the first Agreed Syllabus of Religious Instruction appeared, that it was demonstrated that religious teaching could be lifted above the level of denominational disagreement. It is a depressing reflection that it had taken fifty years for the Churches to find a way of co-operating with the teachers and the School Boards (later, the Local Authorities) and thus begin to make effective the provisions which had been made for the religious education of children in State schools. The price which has been paid, and is still being paid, for this long delay has been heavy indeed.

From 1930 onwards, however, the old controversies had lost most of their significance and public opinion was becoming increasingly concerned about the need for schools to provide an adequate moral education, which, in the light of our educational and religious history, could not ignore the religious question. Thus the 1931 Report on the Primary School made an approving reference to the Agreed Syllabuses of Religious Instruction which were becoming widely used and added: 'The teaching of religion is at the heart of all teaching'. In 1933 the Board of Education summoned a conference, the purpose of which was to consider the need for improved facilities to help teachers to equip themselves for the teaching of religion. Five years later the Report on Secondary Education appeared in which, for the first time in such a document, considerable space was devoted to the whole question of Scripture teaching. One of the most significant passages in this section of the Report may be quoted in full, since it amounts to a re-statement of the traditional English view of the place of religion in general education, and also provides the first clear summary of the educational principles upon which it there rests. It declared:

'It is often maintained that the study of the Bible should have a place in the curriculum for its literary value alone. We do not wish to underestimate that value. The English Bible is one of the glories of the literary heritage bequeathed to the English-speaking peoples. For that reason there is much to be said in favour of the inclusion of portions of the Bible in the syllabus of English literature. But it is also true that no boy or girl can be counted as properly educated unless he or she has been made aware of the fact of the existence of a religious interpretation of life. The traditional form which that interpretation has taken in this country is Christian, and the principal justification for giving a place in the curriculum to the study of the Scriptures is that the Bible is the classic book of Christianity and forms the basis of the structure of Christian faith and worship. The content of the Bible has, therefore, inevitably its own dignity and associations. It can neither be treated merely as a part of English literature, nor can it be merged in the general study of history, though its meaning is, in the first instance at least, historically conditioned.'[1]

Two of the three main reasons why the Education Act of 1944 included specific provisions for religious education in the country's schools have now been noticed. The first might be called the *historical*—the fact that traditionally religion in this country has always been closely linked with education generally. The second we may call a reason of *educational principle* and has never been better expressed than in the passage quoted above from the Spens Report. There was, however, a third reason which may be called, quite simply, the *utilitarian*. That is to say, in the 1930's and early 1940's considerable concern was shown in this country about the evident need of better moral education for the children who were to be tomorrow's citizens. The opposition between the values inherent in our democratic way of life and those which had manifested themselves on the one hand in Nazism and on the other in Communism, itself made apparent the need for re-affirming and re-stating to the younger generation the nature and the basis of the values which form the founda-tions of democratic society as we in the West understand it. Children had to be shown the nature of, and the need for, the attitudes and beliefs which were inherent in good

[1] Op. cit., p. 208.

citizenship as the democracies understood it. And because during the whole course of English history morals and religion had been so intimately associated in private and national life, it was to religious education that people looked primarily to assist in this task of re-defining and re-inforcing personal and social moral values and standards in the minds of the children who would pass through the nation's schools. The Government White Paper *Educational Reconstruction,* published in 1943 as a preface to the Education Bill, expressed this point quite clearly when it said:

'There has been a very general wish, not confined to representatives of the Churches, that religious education should be given a more defined place in the life and work of the schools, springing from the desire to revive the spiritual and personal values in our society and in our national tradition. The Church, the family, the local community and the teacher—all have their part to play in imparting religious instruction to the young.'[1]

A later publication by the Ministry of Education, called *Citizens Growing Up*, referred at much greater length to the need for a religious faith if personal and social values were to be effective in the education of the young.[2]

There has been some criticism of this assumption that the moral education of children should be so closely linked with religious education. From the Christian side it has been said that it suggests a debasing of religion, which ought to be taught for its own sake and certainly not as a means of buttressing up the moral fabric of society. From the secular humanist side has come the objection that it weakens the effectiveness of moral education in the minds of those adolescents who will leave school without religious faith, to be given the impression that moral obligations and

---

[1] Cmd. 6458, H.M.S.O., para. 36.
[2] Ministry of Education Pamphlet No. 16, H.M.S.O., 1949, pp. 9–11 and 36–8. See also the earlier Report of the Central Advisory Council for Education in England, *School and Life*. H.M.S.O., 1947.

principles are mainly the concern of the religious person.[1] This is a large and complicated question which is to be given the fuller consideration it deserves in a subsequent volume in this series. In fairness, however, to those who were responsible for encouraging the view that the provisions for religious education in the 1944 Act were important, among other things, for the sound moral education of children, two facts should be remembered. There is no doubt that at the time a majority of parents would certainly have regarded religious education as the normal and proper framework for a great deal of teaching about personal and social values. Secondly, Christianity has been inextricably involved in the whole complicated business of private and social morality ever since the publication of the Edict of Milan in 313 A.D., at which point it became officially recognised as a State religion. In England, the fact of a 'national church' has served to deepen and complicate this involvement and only those with no sense of history could seriously imagine that religious and moral education could ever be completely dissociated. Probably nobody really does think this. What the secular humanist critics are concerned about is the rather different assumption that the two can be completely identified.

Here then, were three reasons why the Education Act of 1944 included specific provisions concerning religious education in all schools. The actual provisions largely follow the lines of earlier legislation while at the same time adding certain features which appear for the first time. Thus, the safeguards of the 1870 Cowper-Temple clause are retained and it is explicitly stated that neither the religious instruction nor the ordering of the corporate act of worship are to reflect beliefs or practices which are distinctive of any particular formulary or denomination. It continues the earlier

[3] See, e.g., the article in the *Hibbert Journal*, Vol. LIV, October 1955, by H. J. Blackman, 'Religion as Reaction'. Mrs. Margaret Knight's broadcasts, printed in the *Listener*, January 13th, 20th, 27th, 1955, under the title 'Morals Without Religion', represent a similar point of view.

arrangement by which parents can withdraw their children, if they so desire, from the religious instruction lessons or the act of worship, or both. It also reflects the earlier conviction that the Bible shall be the basis of the teaching to be given. That it did not need to be explicit about this point was due, of course, to the fact that the Agreed Syllabuses of Religious Instruction were in general use in the early 1940's and had of themselves solved this particular problem. The legislators of 1870 were in a far less straightforward position in this respect than their successors in 1943–4.

At two points, however, deliberate changes were made in the earlier legislation. Earlier provisions for religious teaching had stipulated that it should take place at the beginning or end of the school day. This stipulation was omitted from the 1944 Act, with the result that since then it has been able to take a more normal place in school time-tables, with some gain to the prestige and effectiveness of the teaching. Secondly, whereas previously such teaching could not be inspected by H.M. Inspectors, the 1944 Act expressly stated that it should be. This change has also had beneficial results.

It has been, of course, some of the new elements in the 1944 legislation which have been most criticised. The Act expressly stated that religious teaching and the provision of a daily corporate act of worship were to take place in all schools, whether county or voluntary. Since 1870, it will be remembered, Parliament had left the School Boards, and later the Local Authorities, to decide what, if anything, should be done in this matter in the schools of their own areas. Indeed, to be precise, the earlier legislation had dealt with religious teaching only, and said nothing about school worship. It has often been remarked that these are the only aspects of the school curriculum which are compulsory and to many it has seemed odd that this should be the case at a time when, by and large, religious beliefs and affiliations seem to attract only a minority of the people of this country. Perhaps there is some excuse for those who have therefore seen in this particular aspect of the 1944 legislation the results of the pressure of the Churches to try to gain ground which they had lost. Historically, however, this kind of criticism is wide of the mark. It has been shown earlier that in the years immediately preceding the passing of the Act there existed widespread and genuine anxieties about the lack of religious and moral teaching in the education of young people. The Agreed Syllabuses were a clear indication that the Churches had put aside earlier disagreements about basic Christian teaching. The element of compulsion in the Act with regard to religious teaching and worship reflected rather the nation's determination that now that something could be done, it should be done, and done well and systematically.

At the time of the debates on the Bill fears were expressed that to make worship and teaching compulsory would result in dull teaching and mechanical school services. The evidence which has accumulated since 1944 suggests, on the contrary, that greater care and thought are being given both to the arrangement and conduct of the School Assembly and to the religious lessons in the class-room, than at any time since the State became officially responsible for educational arrangements. It has also had beneficial effects in other directions. Since religious teaching had to be provided, there has been a growing demand for teachers qualified to teach what is admitted on all sides to be one of the most difficult of all 'subjects'. This has led to the provision of courses in all Training Colleges and in Departments of Education, and so to something like an efficient education in religion of a large number of teachers in the schools. Had the Act not introduced the element of compulsion into this part of the legislation, it is likely that little if anything would have been done about this. To have allowed the old system to continue, under which religious teaching was given by the form or class-teacher in the secondary school, would have meant that little progress would have been made towards better teaching of religion. Now, eighteen years after the passing of the Act, some progress at any rate can be seen, even if a great deal more remains to be done—not least in the grammar schools.

Another important innovation in the Act was the extension of the conscience-clause to the teachers. A teacher could withdraw from the duty of giving religious teaching, or from taking part in the corporate act of worship, or both, on grounds of conscience, without detriment to his prospects and his career. This provision was just as important for the effectiveness of the religious education in the schools as it was for the teachers themselves, since nothing could be worse for religious education than that it should be in the reluctant hands of those who are out of sympathy with it. Whether in practice teachers have always been as free to withdraw as in law they are, is by no means certain. In junior schools in particular, where teachers do not normally specialise in teaching particular subjects, withdrawal presents special problems. That the problems ought to be overcome, in the interest of the Act, of the teachers, and of the effectiveness of the religious education, is evident, as is also the fact that they usually can be, given good-will and understanding on the part of the head and the staff.

An Appendix to the Act set out the procedure which a Local Authority should follow in producing or adopting or adapting an Agreed Syllabus of Religious Instruction for use in the schools in its area. Such a Syllabus is now in use in every area and some Local Authorities have convened a Committee for the purposes of revising an earlier Syllabus. This last point raises the important question whether revision of Syllabuses in other cases is long overdue and will be discussed in a later chapter.

CHAPTER 2

THE CHILD'S RIGHT TO RELIGIOUS INSIGHTS

THERE is told in Boswell's *Life of Johnson* the well-known story of how Dr. Johnson made short work of Bishop Berkeley's philosophical argument that matter exists as an idea in the mind. Johnson struck his foot with mighty force against a large stone, till he rebounded from it and declared: 'I refute it thus'. The teacher who is himself religiously inclined is apt to react rather as Dr. Johnson did when he is asked to explain why religious education should be provided for children in schools. Sufficient justification for him that everyone needs religion and that he himself, as a religious person, is under an obligation to pass it on to others. What more natural than that he should want to see that the children he teaches should know about it too?

This is all quite understandable and natural and yet, in the circumstances in which we find ourselves today, it does not add up to a justification for giving a place to religious education in all schools, and certainly not in those supported by funds provided by the taxpayer. It never has been sufficient justification, in fact, since the Renaissance removed education from the direct control of the Church and began to imbue it with secular rather than religious aims. Increasingly, since then, education has explained itself in terms of principles which are fundamentally those of secular and not religious humanism. When we nowadays define the aims of education as being to develop to the full the abilities and aptitudes of the individual, or to equip him to assume the responsibilities of a good citizen, we are adopting the standpoint of the humanists of the Renaissance who first insisted that the study of man and his activities is a worth-while end in itself. The community nowadays provides schools, not because it wishes the young to be educated ultimately *ad Dei maioram gloriam,* but because the education of the young is a desirable thing in itself and for what we regard as perfectly obvious cultural and material ends. If, therefore, religious education in schools provided by the community for its children is to be justified, it must be on grounds of which the community as a whole, thinking educationally, can approve and not just on grounds which commend themselves to the Christian in the community. Harold Loukes puts the point in a different way in *Teenage Religion* when he says:

> 'The defence of Christian education must be made to rest on the same open ground as that of all our education: it must seek to perform some task which would be accepted as *healthy,* contributing to wholeness of the personality, and and would not be judged by the conscientious agnostic to be limiting or hampering.'[1]

How far can religious education claim, on broad educational grounds of this sort, to be necessary in the education of children?

The first point to be noticed is that recent, small-scale investigations suggest that if a representative sample were taken of the opinions of parents over the country as a whole, it would reveal that a majority were in favour of their children receiving religious education in school. This seems surprising, at first sight, when one remembers that only a minority of adults nowadays are sufficiently attracted by organised religion to want to have direct contact with one or other of the Churches. It seems to confirm the view, often expressed in the Press and elsewhere, that decline in religious belief and observance which has been a marked characteristic of English life since the end of the First World War, is the result of loss of conviction rather than of militant opposition to religion. To put it another way, we live in a

[1] S.C.M. 1961, p. 96.

time of reluctant agnosticism rather than positive atheism. So a good many parents still think it a good thing that their children should learn about religion, and even be brought up to engage in religious worship, in case the children find in religion something which they themselves seem to have failed to discover. This may not be either a very worthy or a very convincing reason, in itself, for continuing to provide religious education in schools, but plainly it cannot be ignored. At least it has this to be said in its favour, that parents who take this kind of view are being objective in their attitude to education. They are adopting towards religion the same kind of objectivity that they might show towards the teaching of other subjects for which they may themselves have little time—possibly Classics, or Art or Music, and so on. From the point of view of the satisfactory development of the child, this kind of objectivity is certainly preferable to the authoritarian attitude of the other kind of parent who wants to determine in advance the child's interests and point of view.

A second and much more significant reason is that education without religion is itself incomplete. Certainly it will be recognised that it would be impossible to introduce young people intelligently to the best of the culture which is their legacy from the past without reference to the religious faith and experience which has often been an integral part of it during practically the whole of our history. This is, indeed, so obvious a fact that it goes almost without saying. Literature, music, painting, sculpture, architecture and much of our social and even our political history have all been profoundly influenced by religion, and can be understood adequately only with some knowledge of religion. Try to leave out all mention of religion and there would be so many large gaps left that the teaching of these subjects just could not make sense to young people.

Much the same is true, not only of the life and thought of past centuries but of life today too. Churches and cathedrals still stand and function; new ones are added to the old.

Artists like Stanley Spencer are still inspired to paint pictures which deal with religious subjects; an Epstein is moved to carve out a figure of the Madonna and Child or Christ in Glory; a T. S. Eliot to deal with important religious issues in dramatic or poetic forms and a Graham Greene to do much the same in his novels. On a different level, the daily Press constantly makes reference to news items which children can understand only with the help of some explanation of re-ligious beliefs or practices—a vote in Wales on the subject of Sunday opening of public houses; a new translation of the New Testament in modern English; controversy about the appointment of Church dignitaries, and so forth. The Christmas or Easter holiday still has a religious background which the majority of people would not wish their children to lose sight of and the Harvest Festival is still a popular annual church-going occasion, to say nothing of weddings and christenings. If, then, education aims to help children to understand the life around them, religion must be brought in.

But education tries to do much more than this: it also aims at helping children to begin to enter for themselves into the best of the experiences which civilised men and women have learned to value. They are encouraged to discover and explore for themselves the resources of the intellect—to store up important facts, to examine, to understand, even to begin to explore fresh avenues of thought. Through art in its various forms they are to discover the meaning of aesthetic experience and to taste the pleasure it can give. Games and dancing and physical exercise generally are provided in order to encourage healthy physical development and, for some, to provide the incentive and satisfaction of attaining prowess in these spheres. We encourage them to learn to master a craft or crafts, that they may know the satisfaction which creative manual work, stemming from a deep instinctive urge in man, can give them. Are we then to try through education to introduce children to all these different aspects of human activity and experience which civilised men have come to think important and yet to stop short at showing them what religious experience has to give to human life? To do this would be, to say the least, unrealistic and illogical. In the light of the fact that religion has brought some of the profoundest and most far-reaching experiences of all, to fail to draw children's attention to what it has to offer them would be totally indefensible. The authors of the Spens Report spoke sober truth when they declared that 'No boy or girl can be counted as properly educated unless he or she has been made aware of the fact of the existence of a religious interpretation of life'. Education which shies away from the imaginative presentation to young people of what religious faith and experience has to offer them is failing in an important part of its task.

It could, of course, be argued that the presentation to the child of this aspect of experience is best left to the parents and the Church. But this is an unrealistic attitude to adopt in the light of prevailing conditions. We noted above just how impossible it would be to omit mention of religion from a good deal of the formal teaching which goes on in the school, so that some discussion of it is bound in any case to play a part in a good deal of teaching apart from a specific 'religious knowledge' lesson. In any case, young people are particularly interested in religion and would certainly expect a good teacher to be ready to be questioned about it. A teacher who habitually refused to discuss it would quickly forfeit the respect of adolescents. But it is also an unrealistic attitude to adopt chiefly, of course, because the majority of children are unlikely, in fact, to learn about religion in the home or the church. The majority of parents, as was made clear earlier, seem to experience more perplexity than conviction about religion and the Churches make contact with only a small proportion of children. The school is the one agency through which religion can be presented to all children at the present time.

This is not to suggest that the schools can, in this matter, completely fill the gap left by the lack of religious influence on the part of parents on the one hand and the Churches on the other. Most educationists would agree that the real roots of young people's beliefs and moral values do in fact need to be nourished in the deeper soil of the more personal life of the home, and, if they will, the church. There is clearly a limit to what the schools can do to remedy the lack of this kind of nourishment and this fact must be faced if religious education in schools is not to be asked to achieve the impossible. Nevertheless, the schools can do something—in certain circumstances they may be able to do quite a lot—for the religious life of children. They can enlighten them about, and arouse their interest in, the Christian faith and way of life which have been the traditional sources of belief and moral standards in this country for almost the whole length of its history. Then, at least, young people will be in a better position to discover whether these beliefs and practices have any meaning for them. If at the same time they observe that religious convictions and practices have a place in the attitudes and behaviour of some of the adults who mix with them and teach them in school, and that the life of the school community is influenced by them, then the school may be going quite a long way to fill the gap which may be left by home and church.

It will be observed that the word 'religion' has now been qualified for the first time in the argument by the addition of the word 'Christian'. This was done deliberately and for a reason which also needs elaborating from an educational standpoint. In this country (as indeed with many other European countries, and those outside Europe which have developed mainly under European influence) Christianity has been the dominant religious influence. All education begins with the attempt to understand the culture and life which is part of the child's own immediate environment. *English* language, literature, history, geography, games, music and so on, with suitable additions at later stages, rightly provide the main sources of the curricula of English schools. It is thought less important, and with good practical reasons, that English children should spend time on the languages, literature and culture generally of, say, Egypt or Persia, India or China. So with religious education, which mainly takes the form of teaching about, and worship in the tradition of, Christianity. Those who suggest that this is too narrow an idea of religious education, or even that it amounts to indoctrination, and argue that children ought to be taught about religion generally, are not only being impracticable, they are also asking that a radical departure should here be made from what is normal educational practice.

This is not to suggest that young people in the upper part of secondary schools should not learn something about the other great religions which attract millions of people in other parts of the world. On the contrary, there is every reason why they should. This should be done, however, after they have first had the opportunity of gaining some insight into the meaning of religion as it has been understood and interpreted within their own culture and tradition. It is in its Christian form that religious faith and experience will most obviously make any appeal that it is to have to them. It is hardly to be expected that many of them would be likely to become practising Muslims, Buddhists or Hindus, however much sympathy with and interest in other men's faiths they may later come to have. 'Indoctrination' of a sort this may perhaps be, but then all education is inevitably a form of indoctrination, not least in this second half of the 20th century. A belief in the freedom of the individual, for instance, seems so important to the peoples of the free world that they would regard their education as failing badly if it did not inculcate the same belief in the minds and hearts of their young people. But we know very well that this is a conviction which has to be taught positively and vigorously in the face of tyrannies of one kind or another which have threatened the free world almost continuously since the 1930's. We 'indoctrinate' similarly, in the matter of generally acceptable standards of behaviour, knowing full well that anti-social behaviour cannot be tolerated in a well-ordered community. The kind of indoctrination which is educationally repulsive to us is that which aims at foisting upon the individual a point of view without giving him as full a picture of all the salient facts as possible and the freedom to come to his own conclusions. All we then require of him is that his point of view be not inimical to the freedom and well-being of others in the same community. It is just this kind of information about the facts of religion, together with the freedom to make up their minds about their implications, that religious education is concerned to ensure for young people. A columnist in a daily newspaper some years ago put the point well in commenting on criticism of religious teaching in State schools, when he wrote:

'Religion is not merely a *feeling,* something you either have or haven't. It is also a great literature, a vast body of doctrine and learning. To make up his mind about all this a child must know something of it. And what can he know if nothing is taught? All men are free to say that science is bunk and economics tripe. Those who may be listened to are those who show some nodding acquaintance with what they are talking about. Similarly, knowledge of religion is not a bar to making up one's own mind about it, but the essential first step towards it. Religious education is not slavery, but compulsory freedom.'[1]

[1] *Daily Telegraph,* January 3rd, 1957.

CHAPTER 3

RELIGION CAN BE TAUGHT

IN what has been said so far it has been assumed that an important part of religious education is concerned with teaching children certain facts about religion—facts, that is, about the Bible, Christian beliefs, and the Christian life generally from the 1st century to the present day. A glance at any Agreed Syllabus of Religious Instruction will show just how much time is expected to be given in the classroom to the imparting of knowledge of facts of this kind. Just how important is this kind of teaching in religious education? Is it the best way in which to arouse children's interest in the faith and experience which lie at the heart of real religion? Is it, in fact, merely teaching *about* religion, rather than teaching religion itself? Can religion, indeed, be taught at all? These and similar questions are often asked with great sincerity by teachers and others who are concerned at the possibility that much of what passes for religious education in schools amounts too often merely to a lifeless, irrelevant recounting of information about the Hebrews and the early Christians, which fails to open the eyes of young people to the nature and significance of religion itself.

That religious teaching in schools does sometimes seem to adolescents to have been not much more than a protracted visit to a museum (and a not very interesting museum at that), is borne out by some of the facts recounted in the book *Teenage Religion* to which reference has already been made —facts which are confirmed in the experience of quite a number of teachers. In order to keep a sense of proportion in this matter, however, it is well to remember that other aspects of the teaching provided by the schools can just as easily suffer from a similar deadness. The teaching of literature, science, mathematics, geography, history, art or music can all become, in certain circumstances, little more to the pupil than dry, dull, dusty catalogues of facts which seem to have little bearing upon life as individual adolescents visualise it. Evidently this was what the study of history, for example, had meant to Henry Ford who, even at the age of 56 declared that 'History is bunk'. And the philosopher Hegel remarked, sourly, 'The one thing one learns from history is that nobody ever learns anything from history.' On the other hand, we can recall that some of the great men of English history, the Pitts, the Cecils, the Cannings and the Disraelis, would not have been the men of vision that they were had they not possessed the broad perspective which they had gained from a wide knowledge of history. One of England's greatest Prime Ministers in our own time has himself testified to the fact that he educated himself by studying history[1]. The point here is, of course, that we cannot condemn the teaching of history or any other subject because it is sometimes taught badly, and that goes just as surely for the teaching of religion.

Another point by no means to be overlooked is that teaching about religion is probably the most difficult aspect of the work which any teacher can be asked to undertake. There are a good many reasons for this, some more, some less obvious. Religion deals with so many imponderables and has so few facts to offer which seem to be capable of straightforward verification that, compared with the teaching of literature, or history, or the sciences, it seems vague and subjective and indefinite. The difficulties involved, for instance, in bringing a class of 14-year-olds to appreciate the types of characters portrayed in a play of Shakespeare, or the results of the Industrial Revolution, or the composition of air, are certainly less formidable than helping them to see what lay behind the prophet Isaiah's sense of the 'call' of God, or the

[1] See *My Early Life*. Sir Winston Churchill, London, 1930.

meaning and implications of the Beatitudes. Moreover, there is plainly a limit to what even the best teacher can do to make religion 'simple': as the French theologian Renan once remarked: 'A religion as clear as geometry would arouse no love and no hate.' Poetry might be easier to understand—in one sense—if the ideas and experiences of which it speaks could be expressed in prose, but then it would no longer be poetry. Religion must preserve, in the right sense, its 'mysterium', even in Lower IV B, or else it will cease to be religion. Then there is the (supposed) lack of agreement among religious people themselves as to what actually are the facts of belief, on the one hand, and the practical obligations, on the other. What is the teacher to say about heaven and hell, the 'fall' of man, the Virgin Birth of Christ, the resurrection, the 'Holy Spirit', miracles, or divorce, war, gambling, apartheid, and the rest? In no other aspect of teaching is he apparently left with so little clear-cut information to give on so many basic matters. Probably his most acute difficulty initially, however, lies in the complex and confusing nature of his basic 'text-book'. Nothing about the Bible, he soon discovers, is quite so straightforward as it appears to be on the surface. Part of what purports to be Hebrew 'history' is not history but legend or myth. Even the more historically reliable parts of the Old Testament are not historical in the sense in which the modern historian would use the term. The book of 'Isaiah' is not all from Isaiah; the Gospels were not necessarily written by the apostles whose names they bear; St. Luke's 'history' is not always historically accurate; and in any case what seem to be biographies of the life of Jesus are in all probability nothing of the sort! In the face of such a formidable list of obscurities and uncertainties about the nature of the book from which most of his religious teaching is to be given, a teacher may be forgiven if he decides to 'stick to something more straightforward' and leave religion to those on the school staff who 'have strong convictions' and know where they stand.

For some people there is a yet more fundamental problem

about the teaching of religious knowledge than all these. They believe that religious experience, the whole religious attitude which makes such experience possible, is something which is communicated, not by teaching of the sort commonly called 'religious knowledge' or 'religious instruction' and so on, but through personal contact at a deeper level. They are concerned that adolescents, at any rate, should be made aware that religious faith and experience involve an orientation, an integration of the whole personality—a kind of insight—which gives a particular kind of meaning and sense of purpose to life as a whole. As the beauty of a flower or of a sunset, they would argue, or the significance of a poem or a symphony, can never be communicated through a verbal analysis of its components and a list of its qualities but has in the last resort to be intuitively apprehended, even more so with religion. Teaching about the Hebrew prophets' experience of God, or about Jesus' life and ministry, or Paul's conversion, can be no substitute ultimately for the kind of intuitive awareness of God which it ought to be the aim of religious education to awake in the child. And when it comes to teaching children about the history of Israel, or the Synoptic Problem, or some of the early Christian heresies, they feel that this really is too much! How, they wonder, can this be justified on any grounds, as being religious education in the real sense of the term? So they conclude that much of what passes for religious education in schools is nothing of the sort:

> Now God forbid that Faith be built on dates,
>   Cursive or uncial letters, scribe or gloss,
> What one conjectures, proves, or demonstrates:
>   This were the loss
> Of all to which God bids that man aspire,
> This were the death of life, quenching of fire.[1]

With the basic point of view here implied, most thoughtful religious folk would agree. Religious faith and experience

[1] Robert Hugh Benson, *Christian Evidences,* quoted from The Oxford Book of English Mystical Verse. Oxford, 1917, p.518.

are ultimately the outcome of an intuitive awareness which a person cannot be 'taught'. In this sense there is truth in the cliché that 'Religion is caught and not taught.' Indeed, the history of religion, and certainly the history of the Christian religion, from the conversion of St. Paul to that of Sadhu Sundar Singh, from that of St. Augustine to that of William Booth, underlines this basic truth. St. Augustine in particular is a notable case of a man who had known and subscribed to orthodox Christian teaching before undergoing conversion in the deeper sense. But this important fact needs to be set over against another, namely, that the Christian view has always been that the individual's intuitive awareness and experience of God is to be developed through, and if necessary corrected by, the greater stream of religious faith and experience which began with and lives on in and through the Christian Church, itself growing out of the even more ancient religious experience of the Hebrew people. These two facts are complementary, not contradictory. The deeper a person's knowledge of the religion of Israel, its shortcomings as well as its permanently valuable insights, the fuller his understanding of the faith which gave birth to the new and vivid religious experience of the early Christians now embodied in the New Testament. The wider his awareness of all that has gone to the making of the history of Christian experience since the close of the New Testament period, the deeper and firmer can the roots of his own faith and experience go down. It is well to remember that among the recognised categories of officials in the Church of the 1st century were the 'teachers', of whom St. Paul could declare that they were just as truly 'called' to that function as were the apostles and prophets to theirs. As a religion which is centred in belief in God's self-revelation in history, Christianity has always insisted that the experience of God in the life of the individual must have its roots in the broader faith 'once delivered to the saints'. It has frequently been pointed out that Christianity knows nothing of a purely individual and isolated faith. In the Christian view, therefore, teaching about religion in this broader sense there must be, as an adjunct to individual religious experience itself.

The distinction between teaching religion and teaching about religion, used so far as a rough and ready contrast, needs to be looked at rather more carefully, because it must not be pressed too far. Every experienced teacher is aware that at certain points what is called 'teaching about' something has passed subtly over into a deeper and more intuitive awakening, on the part of a group of children, or of individuals within a group, of the sort to which reference was made earlier. The great Edward Thring of Uppingham points to this deeper kind of teaching as the ideal:

> Pouring out knowledge is not teaching.
> Hearing lessons is not teaching.
> Hammering a task is not teaching.
> Lecturing clearly is not teaching.
> No mere applying of knowledge is teaching.
> Teaching is getting at heart and mind, so that the learner begins to value learning, and to believe learning possible in his own case.[1]

The awareness that he is 'getting at heart and mind' is by no means an everyday experience, even for the most gifted teacher, but most teachers are occasionally aware that they have 'broken through', as Rick Daladier puts it in Evan Hunter's *Blackboard Jungle*. Rick has read to class No. 21-206 the story of the Fifty-First Dragon and is astonished and elated at the way in which first one boy and then another begins to explore the implications of the story for life as he sees it:

> 'He sat at his desk, and the kids crowded round him, and they asked him if there were other stories like that, where you could get something else out of them and not just the story. And one kid thanked him for showing him the second story about the knight, and it was like finding something special, a present you didn't know was there. . . . '[2]

[1] Quot. E. B. Castle. *Moral Education in Christian Times*. London, 1958, p. 319.

[2] London, 1955, p. 229.

Autobiographies sometimes reveal the extent to which a gifted and respected teacher can influence the development and outlook of young people. Dr. C. A. Alington, Headmaster of Eton from 1916 to 1933, and afterwards Dean of Durham, refers in *A Dean's Apology*[1] to Bertram Pollock's influence upon boys at Eton, where Pollock was a master before coming Master of Wellington College:

> 'His influence over the sixth forms which he taught was astonishing — a fact all the more remarkable because (apart from Theology and the Classics) he was conspicuously ill-read . . . of the reality of his influence it may be enough to say that when I and five of my contemporaries went with scholarships to Oxford, we formed ourselves into a Club called the Hexagon, with the motto "We are seven" . . . (Pollock) was the first person to show me in words the intimate connection of life with religion, and that is a service for which I can never be sufficiently grateful'.

Tributes of a similar kind to the influence of their teachers upon them could be multiplied many times over from the testimonies of men and women from all walks of life, and would doubtless be echoed by many others who were not moved to write their autobiographies. Those whose teaching requires them particularly to try to introduce young people to the world of aesthetic, moral and religious values, rather than to more strictly factual matters, inevitably find more occasions for 'getting at heart and mind' than do some of their colleagues. Certainly those whose task it is to talk of religion must expect to do so.

It is fortunate that, for this particular task, the Bible, in spite of the initial difficulties of presenting it to which reference was made earlier, is an eminently practical textbook of religion. For religion in the Bible is living religion; religion seen at work in the convictions and actions of men and women, not in terms of abstract doctrines or formal worship. And this is as true of the Old Testament as of the

[1] London, 1957, p. 27.

New. Abraham travels from Haran to Canaan because of his strong religious convictions; Moses leads the Hebrew tribes out of Egypt; David establishes a Hebrew kingdom; Solomon builds a Temple; Amos condemns religiosity which has little connection with social and personal morality; Isaiah calls Hezekiah to face Assyrian threats by the strength of his faith in God; Jeremiah suffers for his faith in God. Jesus 'comes into Galilee preaching the gospel of the kingdom'; dies; rises from the dead; thousands in the Roman world are converted by the preaching of Peter, Paul, Barnabas and others; and the early Christian communities stand out vividly, hoping, fearing, working, worshipping, from the pages of Paul's letters to them.

It is true, of course, that all this concerns religion at work, not today, but in the past and in the lives of men and women who lived in earlier types of society, often thinking and seeing life differently from people today, not least because they belonged to a largely pre-scientific era. But once allowance has been made for these differences, it is seen that many of their religious convictions and attitudes and experiences, frequently described powerfully and vividly, still go today straight to the heart of what religion is and implies. The teacher who has known for himself the continual transition which the Bible thus makes for its reader from the past to the present is in no danger of teaching it as if it were a book only about the Hebrews or the first Christians. The children he teaches see it 'coming alive' in a two-fold sense — alive in the way in which he brings Hebrew and early Christian religious views of life vividly before their eyes, and alive in the further sense that it underlines facts, truths, and experience which are as valid for and relevant to the 20th century as they were for the 14th or 8th centuries B.C. or the 1st century A.D. Here teaching 'about' religion passes imperceptibly into teaching religion itself; and, one need hardly add, with none of the 'moralising' which used to be characteristic of scripture teaching thirty or forty years ago.

The historical method of interpreting the Bible, which

scholarship in the last fifty years or so has made possible, itself highlights the permanently valuable elements in the Bible in a way which makes their contemporary significance fairly obvious. Thus, the more clearly the character and work of Amos is seen in its historical setting in the Israel of the 8th century B.C., the more apparent it becomes to young people that the prophet has his successors down the centuries even to modern times. They can see how men like St. Basil, St. Vincent de Paul, Charles Kingsley, William Wilberforce, Father Basil Jellicoe, Trevor Huddleston and others, whose campaigns for social justice have been inspired by their religious convictions, stand in the direct line of succession to Amos. So also can they perceive that a St. Stephen in the 1st, or a Pastor Niemöller in the 20th century, have shown the same determination as the prophet did to preach God's truth in the face of all opposition. Similarly, reasonably intelligent fourteen-fifteen year-olds and their seniors can understand how Second-Isaiah's poems about the Servant of God, whose sufferings bring blessings to others, set a new value, not only upon the suffering Messiah as the first Christians saw him, but also upon the patient suffering of other humbler servants of God since. Even such an apparently mundane historical fact as the emergence of the synagogal type of worship during the years of Judah's exile in Babylon, underlines the significance of simple, spiritual worship as against the more elaborate ceremonials which have been an inseparable part of developed religion the world over.

With the New Testament, the transition from Christian experience in the 1st century to that of the 20th is not difficult to make. For much of the teaching of Christ is in the form of sayings and parables which are full of analogies drawn from human relationships, attitudes and emotions, or from the world of nature, which are as much a part of common experience now as they were then. The vivid hyperbole in such sayings as — 'The hairs of your head are all numbered', or 'What shall it profit a man if he shall gain the whole world and lose his own soul', makes as forceful an impact in 20th century England as it must have done when the words were first uttered.

The Bible then, rightly understood, is both old and very new. Those who look upon it merely as a catalogue of past events put themselves in a position rather like that of the man who said that he could see nothing in Shakespeare. In the case of the Bible, both the old and the new aspects of it are required for healthy religious education. The historical experience of Hebrew religion and early Christianity is the source and inspiration of the new. As the foliage of a tree or the leaves and flower of a bulb emerge each year from the roots of the tree or the bulb, so 20th-century Christianity, like all the centuries of religion which have followed the vital, immediate experiences of the first Christians, is animated and inspired by the roots of that living experience which has become embedded in the Bible.

This is the answer to those who want to argue that we might as well take children straight into contemporary religious faith and experience and do away with so much teaching about the Bible. As well argue that a young musician can safely ignore any music composed before the 20th century, or a young artist the work of the Italian or the Flemish schools, or a young architect or scientist the work of any but the moderns! Even more unrealistic and impossible where Christianity is concerned, since without the sharing in that earliest, vivid, vital experience of faith and hope, the young 'religious' would be cut off from his basic inspiration altogether. If there is some truth, then, in the saying that religion must be 'caught', it is equally clear that so far as the Christian religion is concerned, religion must be taught in order that it can also be caught.

CHAPTER 4

AIMS IN TEACHING RELIGION

THE matters discussed so far will, it is hoped, have served
to make it clear what religious education in schools actually
is, and why it is there. It is now necessary to go on to consider
what are its aims and purposes. Certain general aims are
first discussed and then more specific aims which have to be
borne in mind in relation to the work of primary schools
on the one hand, and secondary schools on the other. This
last distinction is necessary because in any discussion about
the aims of education it is necessary to keep a balance
between what may be desirable and what is practicable.
Children are not adults; they are individuals whose
experience of and ability to grapple successfully with
language or ideas or emotion is gradually expanding. The
aims of their formal education at any particular point must
be thought out carefully in relation to the stage of development which they will have reached. This holds good for
religious education just as surely as for anything else — a
point to which the authors of many Agreed Syllabuses of
Religious Instruction were not always sufficiently alive.

It would be difficult to find a better definition of the
overall aim of religious education in schools than that
already quoted from the Spens Report — to make a child
'aware of the fact of the existence of a religious interpretation
of life' — within the context, that is, of the main-stream of
religious faith and experience as it has come down in the life
and culture into which the child has been born. For children
living in this country, this obviously means the Christian
religion. This, it has been argued, is the right of every child,

just as it is a perfectly sound and defensible educational aim which chimes in with the general aims of the schools. It has also been shown that this amounts to 'indoctrination' only to the extent to which that term could be used of all education. It encourages the child to explore the significance of religion in the light of its value for others to whom it has meant something. It provides him with the information and insights which are necessary if he is to come to a decision about it for himself in due course. But it leaves him free to come to a decision and does not attempt to force a decision on him: to do this would be to transgress a fundamental educational principle and would deprive religious activities in the school of the right to be thought of as religious *education.*

This is particularly important in view of the fact that inevitably quite a few of the teachers who engage in the work of religious education in schools are themselves professing Christians and members of a particular church. As individuals they share the evangelistic compulsion which rests upon the Christian in virtue of his claim to be a Christian: 'Woe unto me if I preach not the gospel'. In the pulpit, the Sunday School or the Bible Class there may be good reasons why, if they are so disposed, they can feel free to engage in positive, undisguised, evangelistic activity and seek to persuade others into an acceptance of the Christian faith and way of life. Here people are present in the full knowledge that such an appeal will be made to them; if they do not wish to hear it they will stay away. Some might go on from here to argue that within the context of the denominational school the same conditions operate; in other words, that religious education in such a school can legitimately take on the same evangelistic colouring. This does not necessarily follow. Once the Churches accept responsibilities for the provision of general education, as distinct from a more direct evangelistic task, it would seem that they have to come to terms with wider responsibilities than the purely evangelistic.

However this may be, it is quite clear that a teacher in

a non-denominational school is there as a teacher, even when teaching religion, and not as a preacher. He must therefore reconcile his personal enthusiasm for the Christian religion with those aims and methods of work which the obligations of his teaching profession on the one hand, and his particular teaching post on the other, lay upon him. He is working in a school provided by the community as a whole for a group of children representative of the whole community. In the local authority school the aims of education are such as are approved by the community as a whole. The school, like the community of which it is a microcosm, is a very mixed body. Not only the children but the staff will be representative of various religious attitudes, or none at all.

Ever since 1870 it has been accepted as a principle that religious education given in this kind of context must be of a broader character than that which will be offered in any one denominational context. As was said earlier, the 1944 Act lays it down that neither in the teaching of religion nor in the conduct of the School Assembly must there be any presentation of points of view distinctive of any particular denomination. Here then, one sees at once that religious education in local authority schools has to adapt itself (in one respect at any rate) to the situation in which it is taking place.

It was, of course, precisely because the Roman Catholic Church felt that it could not accept even this much restriction of its freedom to give religious education in the full denominational sense that it felt unable to become a party to the arrangements made for religious education in the 1944 Act. So today it continues to build its own schools, in so far as it is able or permitted to do so, in which religion can be taught and practised without any restrictions from outside. Probably it would be true to say that there are some outside the Roman Catholic Church who still feel that this is the proper line for the Churches to take. There are indications that some Anglicans share this view, though it does not appear to be the attitude of Church of England leaders in the educational field as revealed in various statements and writings from 1940 to the present time. The late Dr. Spencer Leeson's Bampton Lectures, published under the title *Christian Education*[1] and the various writings of Dr. Stopford, the Bishop of London and Dr. Spencer Leeson's successor as episcopal spokesman for the Church on educational matters, represent a much broader and more co-operative attitude. While believing that Church schools can give to the children of Church people an education which is single and unified in its basic beliefs and standards, they accept the fact that the Church has wider obligations of a less precise but no less important kind to take some sort of share in the work of the State schools. This was broadly the position which Archbishop Temple[2] and the leaders of the Free Churches took during the discussions which led up to the religious provisions of the 1944 Act.

The best Christian teachers who engage in the work of religious education in State schools do not find it difficult or irksome to make the necessary reconciliation between their obligations as a Christian and a teacher. They canalise the one, as it were, into the other in an effort to make their contribution to the religious education in the school as attractive, efficient and meaningful as it is within their power to do. The Spens Report carries just this sort of implication in all that it goes on to say about the way in which religion should be presented to children, urging that it should command all the skill, care and enthusiasm that the teacher can bring to it. It is possible, of course, for the Bible to be taught in such a way as to reduce it to the level of a merely literary or historical study. This, the Report suggests, is not enough. It should be presented in such a manner as makes the religious message plain. Here then, is one of the best expressions of what the ultimate, overall aim of the religious

---

[1] London, 1946.

[2] Archbishop Temple declared that the White Paper on Educational Reconstruction, published in 1943, presented 'a glorious opportunity'. See *William Temple*, by W. R. Iremonger, Oxford, 1948, p. 572.

educationist, certainly in a local-authority school, ought to be. To use one's utmost imagination, insight, skill and enthusiasm in order to present to children the importance and possibilities of religious faith and experience, in the hope that they may be aroused thereby to begin to explore them for themselves. Not to seek to persuade them into an acceptance of faith and commitment but so to teach as to hope to awaken an interest which may lead them to want to find out more for themselves.

Oddly enough, there are still some earnest Christian teachers who feel that all this amounts to less than they ought to be doing — who believe that it is their duty 'to bring the children to the point of commitment'. Certainly one may hope, as has been indicated, that as a result of first-rate teaching, some of the children may themselves want to go on and deepen their religious interests and experience in the life of a Christian congregation. But this is a different thing from urging them to do so. The overall aim in religious education should be to seek to teach, rather than to preach, to enlighten rather than to convert. By this means religious education can claim to be an important part of sound education, even though the direction of educational policy and practice is recognised as now being largely outside the control of the Churches. Religion forms part of school life and work, not because of a sort of historical hang-over from pre-Reformation and pre-Renaissance times, perpetuated in the Dual System, but because education itself would be incomplete without religious (in this country, Christian) education.

Thought of for a moment in relation to the other parts of the curriculum, this kind of ultimate aim reveals affinities with those in the Arts (Music, Painting, etc.) and, to a lesser degree, with that in Literature. That is to say, the ultimate aim of the music or art teacher is not just to teach the techniques of singing, playing, or drawing, or painting, or pottery-making. The best type of teacher also hopes that through the teaching some of the children will begin to see the importance of the values which lie behind these spheres of human activity and make such values a permanent part of their experience. To a lesser degree this aim is also true of the teaching of literature, and would no doubt hold good in varying degrees for the ultimate aims of other kinds of teaching as well.

This particular analogy is also useful in understanding more precisely the way in which a teacher's own personal religious loyalties and insights fit into the aim of religious education as it has been defined above. One art teacher may himself be deeply attached to the works of Degas or Monet but he will be careful to try to interest the children he teaches in Michelangelo and Rubens and many other artists besides. A teacher of literature may have made Milton his special concern but he will not take the attitude of the American professor who, asked by a student a question about Shakespeare, replied: 'Sorry, that's outside my province — I'm a Milton man!' At the same time, the fact that a teacher has penetrated more deeply into the style and outlook of a part of his field at a particular point and understands its significance more deeply, means that he can bring to his teaching as a whole greater insight and effectiveness. The teacher who is concerned with religious education is here in a not altogether dissimilar position. His aim is not just to put across to the children his or her own limited appreciation of religious faith and experience but to present to them the main-stream of Christian religious experience in all its breadth. He is not to know whether Tony Smith in 1C or Sheila Jones in Upper IV A may find their way to God along the path of Roman Catholicism or by joining the Society of Friends. His presentation of Christianity must be sufficiently imaginative and sympathetic to allow for and provide some incentive to either possibility. Yet at the same time his own personal position somewhere along the line which connects the various types of Christian religious experience will be extremely important if his teaching is to have depth and carry conviction. It, and it alone, will give to his teaching the sincerity and vitality which will enable the children to get a sense of the importance of religion. This balance between broad tolerance and wide understanding on the one hand, and sincere personal convictions on the other, does not come easily or without experience but to attain it and to shape one's teaching in the light of it must be one of the most important aims of the teacher engaged in religious education.

A third overall aim should emerge naturally out of the teacher's point of view about the Bible, with which something like three-quarters of his actual teaching of religion may be directly or indirectly concerned. It has already been pointed out that it is through the presentation of the living experience which is enshrined in the Old and New Testaments that the teacher will help children to begin to see what religious faith means in people's lives. 'This is what faith in God meant to Amos, or Jeremiah, or Second Isaiah, or St. Paul, or the Christians at Corinth, or even, for Christ himself' — is what the teacher will, by implication, be saying to them, with the further implication — 'Therefore, this is what it could mean to you'. To teach from the Bible in this sort of way, the teacher must have arrived at a clear philosophy of 'The Bible in the classroom'. The Roman Catholic teacher and the Protestant fundamentalist presumably have less difficulty in reaching a clear philosophy of this kind than do those whose studies have convinced them of the need to reconcile the religious message of the Bible with that fresh light on the Bible which the last hundred years and more of scholarly research in the fields of literary criticism, anthropology and archæology have brought. For many teachers, the religious message has to be sought for in a different way: a scholarly interpretation of the Bible must be made to yield its own kind of spiritual insights and values. This is important even when the teacher is not producing lessons which deal explicitly with the growth of the Bible itself. There will be times, certainly with 4th, 5th, and 6th year classes in the secondary school, when the teacher will want to take some lessons of a simple kind on some of the scholarly work done on the Bible and allied fields of study. But even when he is not actually referring to such matters, the point of view which he has arrived at as the result of his understanding of these studies must affect his presentation of the Bible at almost every turn. This is true right down to the lowest class of the primary school. If he does not want children later on to have to unlearn mistaken attitudes to, say, the first eleven chapters of Genesis, then that fact will help to determine what stories, if any, from those chapters go into the primary school syllabus and, if they go in, the point of view from which they are taught. And one could multiply such examples many times over.

Aims of Teaching in the Primary School

If more research had been done into the nature of religious experience in the pre-adolescent child, it would be possible to write with greater insight about the aims of religious education with children from 5 to 11 years. The fact is that we still know all too little about the religious development of young children.

Some of the most interesting work on the religious attitudes of very young children was done by Professor Pierre Bovet and is described in his book (in the English translation) *The Child's Religion*, which was published in 1928. From observing young children, he came to the conclusion that the earliest manifestations of children's religion show themselves in a 'religion of the parents'. That is to say, the child first imbues his parents with the kind of attributes which classical theology attributes to the Deity: he treats them as if they were omnipotent, omniscient and completely good. This stage, Bovet suggests, continues up to about the age of 7 in normal cases. Then the child begins to discover, with something of a shock (Bovet speaks of 'intellectual crises') that the parents are not as all-powerful, all-knowing and completely good as they had been taken to be. This discovery marks the beginning of an important change and is obviously potentially very significant for the child's religious development.

Piaget knew of, and seems to have approved in general of Bovet's conclusions in this field and suggested that his own investigations confirmed them. He gives some examples from his own observations which point to similar conclusions.

If this is to be taken as indicating the normal path of religious experience for the young child, then clearly it implies that there is a fairly definite point at which young children are ready to be introduced to religious ideas, attitudes and language in the more strictly theological sense and that to attempt to do so sooner might be pointless or even positively undesirable. There would, then, be little point in teaching children about 'God', or encouraging them to sing hymns and say prayers which contain references to 'God', in the infant school; this should more properly begin in the junior school.

No doubt a great deal more investigation is necessary before one could be sure that Bovet's and Piaget's assumptions are correct and most teachers would not easily be convinced that there should be no religious education in the more normal sense of the term in the infant school. At the same time it is worth remembering that what we know about the thinking-processes in general of the young child also suggest that up to the mental age of seven, he is not yet ready for more formalised teaching which is based on logical thinking, whether theological or otherwise. Piaget has referred to the 'pre-operational' thinking which is normal for the child up to this stage of his development. By this he means that his thinking is inconsistent and lacking what the adult would call a logical basis. Professor Peel, in his book *The Pupil's Thinking,* quotes Lodwick's example of the reactions of children to some questions he put to them after they had read a short passage about Alfred and the cakes. A 7-year-old replied to his questions as follows:

'Could Alfred cook?
Yes. (Why?) Because he's the king.
(Can every king cook?) No.
(Why could Alfred cook?) Because he can fight.[1]

If this inconsistent, pre-operational thinking is typical, as the educational psychologists tell us it is, of the normal child up to about the mental age of seven, then it underlines the need to make a most careful selection of Bible stories and hymns to be used with children at this stage. Even when carefully chosen, moreover, they should not be expected to convey more abstract religious concepts like that of 'God' (in the theological sense).[2]

Another and more positive point about the religion of the young child emerges, however, from all this. It was well put in a pamphlet which was published some years ago about *The Religious Education of Children under the Age of Seven Years*.[3] 'Religious education of children under seven is not a matter of instruction but of influence.' What Bovet and Piaget have found helps to explain why this is so. The 'religious' feelings of the young child are naturally directed towards adults who give him a sense of security and affection. Next to the parents, the teacher obviously has an important part to play here. The Ministry of Education Handbook on *Primary Education* published in 1959 goes out of its way to underline this point:

> 'Consciously or unconsciously, the values and the standards which the teacher himself acquired through his own experience make themselves manifest to the children and profoundly affect them.'[4]

Besides this close connection between the young child's

[1] London, 1960.

[2] Research undertaken by Dr. R. J. Goldman of the University of Reading, Department of Education, points to similar conclusions. Children who have been given abstract teaching of a highly verbalised kind too soon, have become familiar with the words as words, but not much more.

[3] Institute of Christian Education, 3rd Edition, 1945, p. 12–13.

[4] H.M.S.O. p. 82.

religious attitudes and his relations with adults, these attitudes also find expression in his enjoyment of nature — flowers, birds and animals — in his cherished possessions, in music and dance, painting and drawing. All these things may give rise to experiences and arouse feelings which at a later stage would be linked, in part, with more mature religious ideas and practices. It is for this reason that many teachers bring these aspects of children's life and experience into the worship and other activities of the young child in school.

The period from mental age 7-11 years, however, normally sees the child's thinking progress from the 'pre-operational' to the 'concrete' stage. That is to say, the child learns to classify, to analyse, to compare, and so on. But, as is well known, this kind of development in his thinking is easier for him where concrete material is concerned than when dealing with abstract things. Lodwick's questions about Alfred and the cakes were answered very differently by the children of from 7 to 9 years of age; four children replied as follows:

'Could Alfred cook?'
(a) No. (Why?) Because he was a king and not a housemaid.
(b) No. (Why not?) He forgot all about the cakes. He was a man and that's why he couldn't cook as well as a woman does. A woman is a proper cook.
(c) No. Because he forgot all about the cakes.
(d) Yes. Well he ought to be able to. Well most men can cook a bit. (Could he cook?) No because he did not take any notice of the cakes and let them burn.

These answers reflect not only the junior child's increasing ability to reason but the manner in which he makes use of concrete experience in doing so. Professor Peel comments:

'Thought is internalised action (and for this reason) activity and construction (need to) form the basis of primary education if it is not only to close the gap between actual thinking levels and stereotyped use of words, but also to provide a naturally developed, surely based foundation for the more abstract formal thinking of adolescence.'[1]

Side by side with this development of the child's power to think more consistently goes a continued interest in and regard for persons. The Ministry of Education *Handbook* comments thus on the child in the junior school:

'A desire to be like his elders and to enjoy, however vicariously, their experiences, directs his interests and actions. He wants to be accepted by grown-ups, especially by those whom he likes, and he wants to share in the contemporary scene, to hear of passing events and adult adventures in the world at large.'

Again:

'They are still very sensitive to the opinion of adults, and the praise and blame of a teacher they like is very powerful.'[2]

These insights into the interests and development which are characteristic of the child of junior school age, seem to carry certain implications for the kind of religious education he should have at this stage. Such teaching as he is given, and hymns and prayers which form part of the worship in which he shares, should deal in the main with religion in the active sense, and especially as seen in the lives and characters of men and women. Closely connected with this point is the further fact that whether religion matters to those adults with whom the child is in the closest contact and, above all, the parents, becomes a matter of prime importance for the shaping of the child's own attitude to religion.

A further point may be added, namely that the religious teaching which the child receives at this stage should begin to deal intelligently with questions which the brighter children are beginning to ask and thus help to lay the foundations of an intelligent attitude to the Bible and to religious beliefs and practices. There is some evidence to show that children start from the mental age of twelve onwards to question some of the traditional religious beliefs

[1] Op. cit., p. 87.   [2] pp. 57, 60.

and ideas which they have assimilated. In the case of children with a high I.Q. this, of course, can, and often does, begin as early as the (actual) age of eight years. From the second year of the junior school upwards, then, depending on the ability of the children in any particular group, teachers must not merely expect, but be ready to encourage, the *beginnings* of intelligent discussion of traditional religious ideas and attitudes as the child has encountered them through Sunday school, church, home or school, and, above all, through the Bible. A class of bright children aged 8 years read the story of Abraham being called by God to leave Haran for 'the Promised Land'. After they had talked about where Haran was, and what sort of people Abraham and the others were probably like who lived at Haran about 2000 B.C., one boy asked — 'Could Abraham hear God speaking to him *with his ears?*' In another class of 9-year-olds, some children wanted to know, in connection with the story of the angels who appeared at the empty tomb of Jesus, 'Why do people not see angels today?' At this age, too, children who read in their encyclopædias articles about the evolution of the world, ask, when they read the story of the Creation in Genesis, 'Why does the Bible say the world was made in six days when people say it took thousands of years?

In dealing with questions of this sort teachers realise that in the junior school they are not only laying the foundations of children's later attitudes to the Bible and religion but also encountering an important aspect of the living religion of the young child. It is a mistake to imagine that any Bible story will do at the junior stage and that the story itself is the beginning and end of the lesson. The stories themselves need to be chosen with an eye to the positive and permanent religious teaching which they contain and the teacher must be ready to explore some of their implications with the children, even at this stage. Fortunately, many Agreed Syllabuses suggest a fair selection of suitable material: others are not so discriminating and need pruning. But not even the best selection of stories can exempt the teacher from the further task of preparing himself for comment on and discussion of particular implications of the stories, by means of which the children can be helped to begin to lay the foundation of a positively intelligent and reverent attitude towards the religious truths to be found in the Bible and in Christian faith and experience generally.

But religious education in the junior school ought to have a further aim. Whether in the Old Testament or in the New, religion is rooted in history — the history of Israel and, finally, the life and ministry of Jesus of Nazareth and the history of the Christian Church. The child of 9-10 years is ready to learn about the 'real' history which lies behind the Bible. What sort of life the Hebrews lived at different times in their long history — the clothes they wore, the food they ate, the houses they lived in, the way they earned their living, or travelled or fought, or worshipped. All this and much more besides, of the 'social history' which lies behind the Old Testament and can help to bring its pages vividly to life, is both interesting and valuable, and should form an important part of the religious education work in the upper half of the junior school. So also should the 'social history' behind the Gospels and Acts in the New Testament. The opportunity for thus making the 'world' of the Bible come alive will not occur again to anything like the same extent in the secondary school, where less time is available and where different aims must take precedence. The child's understanding of the Bible will seldom be quite the same if he does not discover in the junior school this kind of vivid picture of the people who pass across its pages.

That religious education in the junior school is, of course, more than teaching, however important the teaching, is evident. The arrangement and conduct of the daily act of worship is particularly important because the child at this stage accepts it as a normal and natural part of the order of things in a way which is not true of the youngster of secondary school age.[1] Of considerable importance also as we have

[1] Chapter 13 deals more fully with the School Assembly.

seen, are the attitudes to religion which the young child notices in his teachers. Here one comes up against a problem which bothers many conscientious teachers in junior schools more perhaps than it does their colleagues in secondary schools who can more easily opt out of religious education work than can the teacher in the junior school. Just because teachers in junior schools are aware of the kind of demands made upon them by the young child, those who are not themselves practising Christians feel acutely the embarrassment of having to behave, in classroom and assembly, as though they were. This problem is discussed more fully in the next chapter and it is sufficient to say here that the teacher should be guided more by the educational needs (in the broadest sense) of the children and less by the desire to project his personal, adult point of view about religion into his relations with the children. What is ultimately at stake here is the children's freedom to develop their religious ideas and attitudes as the teacher himself has been able to do. They will reject religion soon enough later on, if they find no meaning in it. At the very least they must be given the chance to reject it out of a reasonably full understanding of what it actually has to offer.

AIMS OF TEACHING IN THE SECONDARY SCHOOL

A double aim characterises the best kind of religious education in the secondary school. On the one hand it should make possible a deepening and enlarging of the adolescent's existing religious experience and, on the other, it should lay the foundations of more mature, adult religious ideas, attitudes and experience. In practice these two aims are rarely distinguishable, the latter usually providing the means by which the former is also achieved. Occasionally, however, an experienced and discerning teacher becomes aware that to press upon a particular child a more mature attitude to, for example, the miracle-stories in the Bible, or prayers for the healing of the sick, may have undesirable repercussions upon the child's religious faith as it exists at that time. Cases of this sort usually occur where the child's family are active members of a particular type of Church and they need to be handled with sympathy and understanding.

This illustration also serves to underline another important factor which characterises much of the work of religious education at the secondary school stage, namely, the adolescent's growing awareness of self. The fact that adolescents are usually taught in groups of 20/30 until they reach the VIth Form makes it all too easy for the inexperienced teacher to overlook the fact that from the period of middle adolescence onwards these youngsters need to be treated increasingly as persons in their own right. There clearly are limits to which this fact can influence the methods of teaching but within these limits every effort should be made to encourage individual comment and questions and some attempt be made to know and begin to understand the situation and attitudes of the individual youngsters with whom the teacher talks about religion. With classes in the last year at school, and with VIth Forms, this kind of approach to religious education is absolutely essential.

The secondary school teacher quickly becomes aware that one of the more obvious ways in which this heightened sense of individuality may show itself in some adolescents is in an apathy about and even overt hostility to religion. This is in part an inevitable result of the perplexity and uncertainty about religious matters which characterise the adult element in our society at the present time and ought to occasion no great surprise:

> The fathers have eaten sour grapes
> And the children's teeth are set on edge.

Clearly this fact, too, will not be without its influence on the aims of religious education in the secondary school. In spite of all the religious education which the 14/17 year-olds may have received in earlier years, the teacher must make continued efforts to help his 4th, 5th and 6th year classes to perceive the importance and the worth of religion, instead of simply assuming that he can build upon a ready acceptance of religious faith and some religious experience. As one grammar school master put it, in describing his work with VIth Forms, he is aware that this may be, for the majority of the boys, their last firm contact with any reasoned and consecutive presentation of religion.

That at the present time a good deal of religious education in the secondary schools is failing to make much impact upon the attitudes of adolescents, or even failing to teach them some of the basic facts which the Agreed Syllabuses suggest should be taught, has been made abundantly clear in two recent investigations.[1] The two main reasons, it is suggested, are unsuitable syllabuses and a lack of well-qualified teachers. These matters are examined in later chapters.

So far as the teaching aspect of religious education in the secondary school is concerned, the first aim must be to teach important parts of the Bible in such a way as to show their contribution to the understanding of religion as the Christian believes in and experiences it. This means teaching parts of the Old as well as the New Testament, for the latter takes much of the former for granted. And since God in Israel's experience is, as has been said earlier, pre-eminently the God who revealed Himself in Israel's history, this in turn means teaching essential parts of the history of Israel as a necessary preliminary to understanding the *religious* message of the Old Testament. But careful selection is essential here, just as it is with the New Testament: how such selection can best be made will be discussed in a separate volume in this series. Above all, whether it be the Old Testament or the New which is being taught, its implications for life at the present time need continually to dominate the teaching if adolescents are going to see any point in it. 'The Bible and Life', to borrow the title of a B.B.C. schools programme on religion, should be the headline which dominates the secondary school teacher's lesson-notes on Bible teaching.

[1] H. Loukes, Op. cit., and *Religious Education in Secondary Schools,* University of Sheffield, Institute of Education. London, 1961.

To lessons based directly and obviously on the Bible need to be added others showing Christianity in action in the various periods of the Church's history from the last century to the present day. In another volume in this series will be found a fuller description of the sort of material upon which the teacher can draw for lessons of this kind.

From the 4th form upwards in grammar schools or streams, and in the last year of the secondary modern school, the teaching should deal directly with life as young people are coming to experience and understand it, rather than with primarily Biblical and allied topics. This is the period at which relations between the sexes, relations with the family, the use of leisure, money, the choice of a job, together with broader social and political issues, are beginning to occupy a larger place in the thoughts and feelings of adolescents. Discussion of the complex issues here involved needs to be encouraged against a background of Christian belief and standards of conduct. For this, continual reference, by the teacher at any rate, to the Bible, Church history, Christian doctrine and Christian ethics, will be essential. It will be the more effective for being unobtrusive and for appearing less obviously the beginning and end of the lesson itself.

Many teachers also feel that this is the time for a more deliberate presentation of Christian belief. If so, it will be essential to deal honestly and frankly with the secular alternatives to Christian belief, perhaps enlisting the help of a conscientious secular humanist on the school staff. The teacher's aim here should be to show how Christian faith offers a positive attitude to life, even if it may not claim thereby to provide a satisfactory answer to all its questions and problems. There is everything to be gained from the attempt to do this over against the secular alternative. This brings an element of hard reality into the teaching for young people who will soon be going out into an adult world in which religion has to hold its own against a good deal of disbelief of one kind or another.

This is also the place in the secondary school course to

deal briefly with the fact of the existence of great religions other than Christianity. Just as it would be unwise to allow young people to get to the end of their schooling without facing up to the existence of secular humanism, so it is undesirable to ignore the fact that Christianity is one great religion (even if normally *the* religion for most Europeans) among several. Once again, this is a large topic which will receive fuller treatment in a separate volume in this series.

The planning of religious teaching in the secondary school along the lines which are here suggested demands the provision of at least two periods of religious knowledge a week for each class. Unfortunately this is by no means standard practice and until it is, the fact has to be faced that religious education in secondary schools is bound to suffer from grave deficiencies, not the least of which will be a lack of esteem in the minds of the young people themselves. Heads who are concerned that the claims of religion should be adequately presented to the children in their school will themselves be anxious to ensure that adequate time is found for it in the time-table.

It should also be remembered that in many secondary schools there exists a voluntary society which meets out of school hours to discuss religion and sometimes to engage in some form of social service as an expression of religious faith. Such groups are, of course, in addition to the formal work of religious education and are in no sense a substitute for the proper provision of teaching time. They have a special contribution to make to religious education in the school and can do much to foster the religious development of young people in a way which may not be possible through the formal life and work of the school. (See Appendix.)

The number of secondary schools presenting candidates for the G.C.E. examinations in religious knowledge at O and A Levels is increasing steadily from year to year. This aspect of the work involves the consideration of matters which are discussed in chapter 12.

CHAPTER 5

QUALITIES AND OUTLOOK OF THE TEACHER OF RELIGION

THE belief still survives, not least among teachers, that the teaching of religion should be left to the practising Christians on the school staff. This is at any rate a more promising attitude than that which used to lead to its being undertaken, willy nilly, by every class-teacher or form-master in the school, since at least it may be assumed that the practising Christian will be unlikely to deal with it in superficial or perfunctory fashion. Clearly it is important that religion should be handled by those who know something of its meaning and value from their own experience: 'Thou canst not speak of that thou dost not know' is a principle which applies with even greater force here than in the context to which Shakespeare applies it. This is true, indeed, of all good teaching, whether it be arithmetic at one end of the scale, or poetry at the other; and of religion it is truer than of any other.

At the same time, it is possible to imagine circumstances in which the earnest Christian may not necessarily always be the best *teacher* of religion. Reference has already been made to the type of enthusiastic Christian who fails to reconcile his strong personal desire to *preach* with his professional obligations as a *teacher*. Usually the preaching of religion which is done by this kind of teacher in the course of religious knowledge lessons is accompanied by a tendency to stress one point of view about religion, or one kind of religious experience, at the expense of others. This can cause resentment among the youngsters who suffer it and may even cause harm. It is obvious then, that more is demanded of the good teacher of religion than merely strong personal convictions about religion, important as these are in their proper place. He needs also to be possessed of wide sympathies which enable him to see the many-sided nature of religious faith and experience. This point has already been touched upon and need not be further elaborated.

He must also be familiar with the most important work of scholars in the field of Biblical studies and allied fields. This is doubly important in an age which finds the Bible a less attractive and certainly less convincing authority in matters of religion than was the case even fifty years ago. Then the divine authority behind the Bible was still widely accepted and so the Bible could be taught largely as it stood. If the Ten Commandments declared that God said: 'Thou shalt not covet — or murder — or commit adultery', then God had so said. Individuals doubtless still transgressed the Commandments but they did not at the same time normally call in question the Biblical authority of the law which they had broken. Now all that is changed and the ironical factor in the situation is that the very scholarly studies which have shed fresh light on the Bible have contributed, in part, to the loss of the sense of Biblical authority. The thinkers of ancient Greece, and particularly Xenophanes and Plato, encouraged men to reflect upon the traditional religion, with the result that 'men climbed Mount Olympus and found no gods there'. Something very like this has happened to religion in England in this century, as the Bible, and with it the Christian gospel which stems from it, came to be looked at through the eyes of the scientist, the linguist, the literary critic, the historian, the anthropologist, the psychologist and the philosopher. What Walter Lippmann calls 'the acids of modernity' have dissolved the religion of our forefathers which, though they quarrelled a good deal as to its details, nevertheless left them in no doubt that there was an order in the universe of which they were a part.

Some might argue that it was a grave mistake ever to have

attempted to look at the old Bible stories and teaching in this scientific and historical fashion. Shaw remarks with great insight in the Preface to *Back to Methuselah*: 'All the sweetness of religion is conveyed to the world by the hands of story-tellers and image-makers. Without their fictions the truths of religion would for the multitude be neither intelligible nor even apprehensible; and the prophets would prophesy and the teachers teach in vain.'[1] But it is certainly vain to wish now that the clock could be put back: just how vain is well illustrated by the futile attitudes and arguments of modern Biblical fundamentalism. What is needed, as was suggested earlier, is that the spiritual message of the Bible should be seen from within a new, intellectually honest appreciation of the literature which makes up the Bible. It is with this task that the best of the Biblical and theological scholarship of the last thirty years or so has concerned itself, and it is the fruits of this task that have to be communicated to young people by their teachers. But in order to be able to do this, a teacher needs not only to be acquainted with the the most important advances in Biblical and allied studies in the last thirty years or so. He needs, even more, to have assimilated them so that for him they have crystallized down into a clear conception of the religious value of the Bible which will pervade his teaching. In the words of the ancient Church of England Prayer Book collect, he needs not merely to have 'read, marked and learned' but 'inwardly digested' it.

A very important part of this process of 'digesting' must be concerned with the interpreting of the Bible in the light of contemporary understanding of Christian beliefs. For it is by this latter yard-stick that the teacher will examine and present to young people the various levels of religious belief and experience which the Bible contains. The Old Testament, for example, contains numerous passages which reflect ideas of God, and man, and of God's dealings with men, which fall well below the level of the Christian belief about

[1] Pelican edition, p. LX.

these matters. The able teacher will be fully aware of this fact and clear about how to explain to children the presence of such passages in the Bible. Within the New Testament also are to be found interpretations of the gospel of Christ which were more significant for 1st and 2nd century Christians than they are for those who have to live in the very different circumstances of the 20th. The, to us, extravagant and artificial use which the author of St. Matthew's Gospel makes of Old Testament 'prophecy' is an obvious example. St. Paul's teaching, in his letters to the Thessalonians and Corinthians, about the early return of Christ, is another. Here again, the able teacher knows how to explain these matters in a sympathetic and positive manner, because he has tried to enter into the background of 1st and 2nd century Christian experience and learned to distinguish its transient features from those which have continued to form essential aspects of Christian convictions down to the present day.

The kind of teaching thus envisaged is not, then, a task to be undertaken by the immature amateur, out of limited personal experience and lack of serious reading of Biblical and theological literature. Those who have so tried, have quickly become aware of the superficial and unsatisfactory character of their efforts as compared with the surer, more informed teaching which they are accustomed to give in the subject, or subjects, in which they are qualified. Even more important, they become aware of their failure to win the respect of the children for their Scripture teaching. Youngsters in secondary schools are too often heard making some such comment as: 'He (she) can teach English (or History—or Physics) alright, but when he (she) takes Divinity, its deadly'—and often, alas, they are quite right.

Some may object that this is to suggest that religion must inevitably become difficult for children, whereas it should be a simple thing. Doubtless there is an utter simplicity at the very heart of religion—the simple trust, as the New Testament reminds us, of the childlike. No doubt too, if we lived in a simpler, less sophisticated era, the presentation and defence of religion would be achieved more simply than it is. But we do not; we live, as was said earlier, at a time when it is demanded of religion that its credentials be those to which a sophisticated and sceptical age can give intellectual assent. So the simplicity with which the religious attitude begins must, for most young people, be justified and buttressed with all the explanation and justification which the able Christian scholar and thinker can command.

In fact, there is nothing startlingly new in this phenomenon: up to a point it has been a feature of Christian preaching and teaching since New Testament times. The Gospel of St. John is itself an example of the way in which some early Christian teachers set forth the Christian gospel in terms which were meant to be attractive to those whose thinking had been influenced by Jewish-Hellenistic ideas. What is new in our age is the extent to which the justification and defence of religion has to try to come to terms with a basic attitude to life which is derived from a reverence for the scientific point of view—the attitude which demands 'facts' which can be 'proved'.

In any case, there is no *prima facie* reason why young people should be deterred by the discovery that the process of justifying, explaining and understanding religion is no less exacting than the task of mastering the insights of history or the principles underlying the differential calculus. On the contrary, religion raises the profoundest issues of all the 'subjects' to which school seeks to introduce them and the wise teacher will prepare them for the discovery that just because this is so, its study will demand more rather than less effort. To this kind of stimulus, moreover, children will respond; what they quickly lose interest in is the wishy-washy, intellectually feeble and unconvincing teaching which sometimes passes for religious knowledge.

As was remarked earlier, one of the encouraging results of the inclusion in the Education Act of 1944 of specific provisions about religious education has been the increased attention given to courses for teachers of religious knowledge in Training Colleges and University Departments and Institutes of Education. In the Training Colleges, students who take a main course in Divinity are able, in three years, to attain a reasonable standard in Biblical and theological studies. The Ministry of Education also makes it possible for experienced serving teachers to be seconded by their Local Education Authorities in order to take a full-time one-year course leading to the award of a Diploma in Religious Education—a course which also reaches a high standard in the academic study of Divinity. The fact that these courses have by no means been fully utilized as yet is itself an indication that teachers could still do more to equip themselves to provide better teaching of religion.

It is in the grammar school field that the shortage of well-qualified Divinity teachers, and especially men teachers, is still most acute. It seems unlikely that in the foreseeable future there will be any large increase in the number of men with theological honours degrees who take up teaching, for the Churches inevitably absorb the majority of them. But there is no reason why an increasing number of intending graduate teachers should not be encouraged to read for a joint honours degree in Divinity and one other field of study. A few universities already provide such courses, including Cambridge through the 'mixed' Tripos. If more universities would offer the same facilities, this would go a good deal of the way towards offering a solution to this particularly urgent problem. It is much to be hoped that the new universities, in particular, will make this kind of course part of their deliberate academic policies. On the practical level there is much to be said in favour of the Divinity teacher being qualified to teach in another field. It overcomes the difficulty which some headmasters and headmistresses see, that specialist teaching of religious knowledge may tend to set religion too much apart from the rest of school life and work. It enables the divinity teacher more easily to gain the respect of the children and of his or her colleagues on the staff because he or she is known and seen to be qualified to teach an 'ordinary' subject. The teacher himself finds intellectual stimulus and relaxation in being able to move over from teaching about religion to the consideration of a more mundane subject.

To these three qualities of the teacher of religion—personal concern about it, broad sympathy about its different manifestations, and some academic study of theology—must be added a fourth, an understanding of life. *Experientia docet* is as true in matters of religion as of other aspects of life. The teacher who knows the real world of men and women outside his own normal channel of school and university, home and church, can bring a sense of reality and conviction into his teaching about religion which an adolescent will notice instantly and respect. H. G. Wells once wrote that if he wanted a 'saviour' he would be more likely to find one in an Oliver Goldsmith, who had tasted the bitter dregs of hardship and suffering, than in the 'pale Galilean' who seemed to him to have passed lightly over the surface of life's troubles. We need not agree with all the implications in his comparison to take his main point—that those who would lead others towards spiritual understanding and insight must themselves know the life that the others really live. This is doubly important if a teacher is to teach religion to young people, because he can be pretty sure that, to begin with, children will assume that he is slightly odd and 'unreal' to be teaching it at all! It goes almost without saying that he will not convince them otherwise by taking school games (though this may help, other things being equal) or by injecting bright and breezy colloquialisms into his religious knowledge lessons. What is needed is that almost unconscious infusion into his teaching, by analogy, anecdote, comment and by general treatment of the 'Bible' lesson, of the sense of *humanity* which springs from experience of life as the majority of folk know it and which brings religion well into the middle of real life without at the same time allowing it to lose its *mysterium*. Since experience in this sense can deepen with the years, it stands to reason that the young teacher often will, and must indeed expect to be at some disadvantage here. Even so, years do not of themselves bring experience and the time spent in a college and in study can, if used to the full, do much to set the maturing process going. A great deal of experience is to be learned through reading and music and painting, through travel abroad in vacations, and through working during vacations alongside people whose own experience has been gathered in somewhat different circumstances. The cultivation in student days of a mind which is open and receptive to the experience which is to be culled from these activities and contacts will enable the young teacher to bring to his teaching, even in the early years, something at any rate of the qualities which can help to make religion seem to children a part of the real world.

So much for the ideal teacher of religion. But what of the situation as it often is, where there are not enough ideal teachers of this sort to be found? The 1944 Act created an immediate need for large numbers of teachers to teach religion. They were not available in sufficient numbers, nor, in spite of the efforts which have been made since then, are they now. In this situation many teachers have found themselves faced with a difficult choice—either to 'opt out', as the Act fully allows them to do, or to do the best that they can in order to avoid disrupting the time-table and absenting themselves in too great numbers from the School Assembly. In junior schools, where class-teaching and not subject-teaching is the norm, these difficulties have often been more acutely felt than in the secondary schools where the R.I. specialist can often be found to carry the teaching load.

In the face of this kind of dilemma some sort of compromise as between the ideal and the practicable is clearly desirable. Even so, that some teachers ought to opt out of the teaching of religion, both for their own sakes and for the children's, is plain. A teacher who is positively opposed to religious belief and practice ought not to allow himself to be put into a position in which he has to act as if he believed otherwise. Probably however, the majority of those who find the present arrangements distasteful come into the category of perplexed agnostics rather than of positive atheists or convinced secular humanists. In their case, if no alternative is to be found, they will doubtless feel that they have to do the best they can. It is worth while their remembering that in any case their task is to teach what *Christians* believe about religion and the Bible, without having to project their own doubts and perplexities into their lessons. Certainly to do this calls, in their case, for great objectivity and very broad sympathy indeed. They find it necessary to study and try to understand Biblical teaching and Christian belief generally while aware that they have not found it convincing themselves. Certainly too, they will derive satisfaction from this part of their work only if they constantly remind themselves that what they are teaching may later on be important to some of the children, even if the teacher himself has not found it so.

To a teacher in these circumstances it may be of interest to recall how T. H. Huxley felt it necessary to take something like this detached, objective view when he was faced, in the London School Board, with the decision whether to throw in his weight for or against the provision of Bible teaching in London schools. For all his own dislike of organised religion, Huxley decided that, just as he allowed his own children to read the Bible, so he had no right to deprive other children of the opportunity of doing so.[1] He was much criticised by some of his acquaintances for taking this stand but remained convinced that it was the right *educational* decision.

When all is said and done, however, this kind of compromise can be but a second-best, both for the teacher and for the children. The fact that it has to be discussed at all

[1] C. Bibby in Article *The First Year of the London School Board*, in Durham Research Review. Vol. II No. 8., September, 1957.

indicates how urgent it is that the supply of teachers who are
interested and equipped to teach religion in the schools
should be considerably increased. This is as important for
the effectiveness of religious education as it is for the freedom of the teachers, for whom the conscience clauses in the
1944 Act should be able to be fully operated in practice.

CHAPTER 6

THE IMPORTANCE OF KNOWING THE FACTS

AT various points in the preceding chapters, emphasis has been put upon the need for presenting to children in a quite objective way the facts of religion. It has been emphasised that this is by no means all that is involved in the teaching of religion—that the teacher who knows from his own experience the value and significance of religion is constantly passing over from the teaching about religion to the teaching of religion itself. Nevertheless, it is with the presentation of the facts of Christian faith and experience, as they emerge in the Bible and the whole 1900 years and more of the Christian tradition, that religious education must be constantly concerned. And it is with the mastery of these facts that the academic studies of the teacher of religion, referred to in the last chapter, are concerned. Moreover, it is just because the more important facts have to be presented to children as the basis for any religious experience, that even the religiously uncommitted (but not unsympathetic) teacher can, if circumstances make it necessary to do so, at least hope to make some useful contribution to religious teaching and not be left with the feeling that so far as he is concerned these lessons must inevitably consist of the projection into his teaching of just his own doubts, reservations and uncertainties.

Religious knowledge lessons probably often fail to gain the attention, if not the respect, of adolescents in particular, just because, by contrast with most of the rest of the teaching given in school, they are sadly deficient in facts and seem to young people to consist more of the ventilating of opinions

72

and attitudes. Adolescents in these days tend rather to share the view expressed by Mr. Gradgrind in Charles Dickens' novel *Hard Times*: 'Now what I want is facts. . . . Facts alone are wanted in life'—especially when their minds are beginning to turn towards the prospect of leaving school and earning their own living.[1] In earlier years, as was pointed out in a previous chapter, abstractions about religion have little hope in any case of meaning much to the child—facts, on the contrary, have and can.

Hence—the teacher must know the facts. But what sort of facts?

Broadly speaking, there are three different kinds of facts which the teacher ought either to know or, at least, know where to find. The most straightforward of all are the historical or actual facts about Christianity itself—past and present. Of these there is, of course, practically no end but some are more important than others and some are essential for the understanding of how Christianity has become what it is today. A few examples of these last may be given: they and others will be considered at greater length in a later volume in this Series which will deal with *The Churches*.

Christianity was not a new religion—it began as a movement inside Judaism but soon became a world-religion. A few dates are extremely important for the understanding of the kind of world in which it began and the way it expanded. Jesus himself was probably born between what we now call 7 and 5 B.C. and not in the year which (in the 6th century) was fixed as the year of his birth (1 A.D.) St. Paul, through whose efforts above all the gospel began to be preached to others besides Jews, probably died in the persecution of the

---

[1] Some of the comments quoted in *Teenage Religion* bear this out. In a class discussion adolescents said:

'People can write a book saying that so and so did so and so, but that doesn't mean that it is true.'

'In Maths and Science today we don't accept anything until it is proved — we say, if x = so and so, then so and so must = x, and we don't accept it until it is proved! . . .'

'If I hear something, I like to have it proved, and that's why I don't go to church or anything like that.'

Roman Christians started by the Emperor Nero in the year 64 A.D. The way in which a 'New Testament' came into being is important and interesting. It is not generally appreciated that the process was gradual and largely spontaneous and that it went on over four hundred years and more.

To children in English schools the facts about the spread of Christianity in Britain are obviously important—that the first mention of Christians in Britain occurs at the beginning of the 3rd century; that Columba landed on Iona in 563, and Augustine on the shores of Kent in 597. The existence today of what are known as the Orthodox Churches of the East dates from the final separation of the eastern from the western branches of the Christian Church in 1054. Similarly the distinction between what we now call the Roman Catholic Church and the various 'Protestant' Churches began with the Reformation, which reached a decisive point with the excommunication by the Pope of Martin Luther on June 15th, 1520. The Free Churches have their origins in further divisions within the reformed Churches. The Society of Friends, for instance, was founded by George Fox in the 17th century. Children ought to know that the established Church of Scotland is Presbyterian and that there the Anglican Church is in a position comparable with that of the Roman Catholic or the Free Churches in England.

They ought also to know some of the facts about the great missionary movements in the 19th century. The Baptist Missionary Society, for example, was founded in 1792, and the Church Missionary Society in 1799. The World Council of Churches, one of the most remarkable signs of the modern desire for unity among the Churches, is as yet in its youth: it was founded in 1948 at Amsterdam. They ought to be aware that in spite of the atheistic policies of Soviet Communism there is an Orthodox Church in the USSR. That 'Catholic' means strictly 'universal' and not 'Roman Catholic'—as is often implied in popular speech.

Many basic facts connected with the beliefs and practices of the different denominations and sects within the Christian

Church need to be taught. That many of our great English cathedrals were once monastic churches: that the Holy Communion is variously known as 'The Breaking of Bread', 'The Lord's Supper', 'The Eucharist', 'The Mass'. That Seventh Day Adventists keep Saturday as their special day of worship, or that Mormons no longer practise polygamy.

All these and many other equally important facts derive, of course, from a knowledge of what is called Church History. Among teachers of religion this often tends to be a neglected field of study, yet it ought to be apparent that Christianity cannot be fully understood or explained to young people without constant reference to the important aspects of its now nearly two thousand years of history. On the whole, many of the Agreed Syllabuses of Religious Instruction may be fairly criticised for the scanty use which they suggest should be made of the development of the Christian religion from the 2nd century onwards, and particularly in the last fifteen hundred years.

The second kind of facts with which the teacher should be familiar are those about the Bible, to some of which reference was made in chapter 4. It was there suggested that the geographical and historical (especially social) facts about the different periods of Israel's history and about New Testament times should receive prominence in religious teaching. It was further argued that much of this kind of factual teaching could best be done in the junior school. For older children, however, there are many facts of a rather different kind which are of the greatest importance for their understanding both of the Bible itself—its origins, the nature of its literature, its 'authority'—and of its teaching. Here again, are a few examples, taken from a much larger number, with which the teacher must make himself thoroughly at home.

It has become a commonplace to say that the Bible is not a text-book of science, or of history (in the sense in which the word 'history' is used nowadays). It was written by men who lived in a pre-scientific age and whose view of history was dominated, not by a desire to produce an accurate,

'Hansard-like' record of events, but rather, a religious interpretation of the nation's history. We now understand, as our predecessors a hundred years ago did not, that it is the religious message of the Creation-stories in Genesis, not their mythological framework, that is important. We know that it is the religious message which the Hebrews perceived in their history which gives much of the Old Testament its importance in the 20th century and not the vain attempt to see in it a plain record of the external events. Indeed, certain books which appear in the guise of historical material are now understood the better for recognising that their historical shape is merely a cover for the presentation of an important religious message. Jonah and Daniel are the classic examples of this kind, while the Book of Job comes fully into its own when it is seen as the fine poetic work that in fact it is. It is also a fact that the so-called Book of the Prophet Isaiah includes a good deal of material by later prophets: chaps. 40–55 in particular take on a new and profounder meaning when they are set against the background of the years immediately preceding the return of the first Jews from exile, c.540 B.C.

These and many other facts about the Old Testament have been uncovered for us by the work of Biblical scholars over the last hundred years or so. Though present-day scholars would be the first to admit that there is much that still remains to be discovered about the Old Testament and Israel's history, they are agreed about many things. These constitute facts about the Old Testament and the history to which it refers which the teacher needs to understand and make the basis of his teaching. Nor is he to allow these facts to be in the slightest degree obscured in his mind by the handful of well-meaning but perverse fundamentalists who struggle vainly to show that the vast majority of Biblical scholars are leading us astray by means of theories which are without foundation. There exists a society of folk whose aim is to convince us that the world is flat! The 20th century exponent of Biblical fundamentalism comes from the same mould and can be safely left in his uncomfortable cul-de-sac so far as the teacher is concerned.

Archaeology too, has been presenting us with a rather different set of facts which often shed fresh light on the Old Testament. If, on the one hand, archaeologists have been unable to discover the remains of the walls of Jericho in Joshua's time, on the other, they have been able to tell us a great deal about the life of the peoples of the Middle East, and about the Israelites themselves, in the Biblical period. In a rather different sphere, the discovery of the now famous Dead Sea Scrolls has given us copies of the Hebrew text of parts of the Old Testament far older than those which we knew before. Archaeology thus puts into the hands of the teacher a tremendously important collection of facts about the history and religion of Israel which can, if used properly, do much to help young people to realise that behind the pages of the Old Testament lies the story of a people who had a definite place in the ancient history of the Middle East.

With regard to the New Testament too, there are many facts about its composition and the teaching it contains on which scholars have for some time been agreed—even though once again, there are still many others about which they are by no means yet clear. The dates of the composition of the four Gospels and of Acts can be fixed within a few years or so. The use of St. Mark's Gospel by the authors of St. Matthew and St. Luke is evident, as is the fact that even the earliest of these Gospels is not a purely factual record of Jesus' life, ministry, death and resurrection, but rather an account of what the Church was proclaiming about all this thirty years or so afterwards. On the negative side we may be less confident than our forefathers were as to who wrote the Gospels, but on the positive side the facts which have come to light enable us to enter a little more deeply into the minds of those who did finally compose them.

On the whole, archaeology has less to offer us as yet in connection with the New Testament background than it has done for the Old. Even so, some extremely important discoveries have been made, especially of very early Bible manuscripts. We now possess a papyrus fragment which contains part of St. John's Gospel written about 150 A.D.—fifty years or so after the time at which the Gospel was first written. Contrast this short gap of about fifty years with the seven or eight hundred years and more which separate the writing of some of the Greek and Latin classics from the date of our copies of them, and it is possible to see how much nearer archaeology has taken us to the actual New Testament writings than to Plato, Virgil and other classical writings.

Some exciting discoveries have also been made about some of the cities where St. Paul preached which seem to show, among other things, how careful an historian St. Luke tried to be. The remains of a 2nd century altar has been found at Pergamum bearing an inscription in Greek: 'to the unknown gods' (θεοῖς ἀγν[ώστοις]) which is reminiscent of what St. Paul says he had seen at Athens. In the British Museum can be seen a block which once formed part of a 1st century A.D. Roman arch in Salonika (called in the Acts 'Thessalonica'). On it in Greek is a list of city-magistrates who are called 'politarchs'. This is exactly the title which Luke uses in Acts 17.6 to describe the magistrates in Thessalonica, and suggests that he was well aware that the city was a 'free city', and so allowed to have an assembly and 'politarchs' of its own.

Here then, are a few examples of the considerable number of facts about the Bible itself and its contents which the teacher needs to be able to find out and to use in his teaching. They and others will be discussed at greater length in the volume in this Series on *The Bible*. It must be evident that the fullest use of facts like these ought to be made in teaching if only to convince young people that there are in the Bible some 'facts' at any rate which can be 'proved'.

Finally, there is a collection of facts which usually present the teacher with his most knotty problem—facts about Christian belief. At first sight, to use the word 'facts' at all in this context may seem to be a misnomer. Yet, in the most obvious sense, facts of belief there certainly are. The Creeds confirm this, for they are summaries of traditional Christian belief. But behind these plain facts of Christian belief lie others and it is chiefly with these that these next paragraphs are concerned, because they are extremely important and yet at the same time less widely known and referred to than they ought to be.

In the various epochs of Christian history Christian teachers have explored the implications of the beliefs summarised in the Creeds and tried to elaborate them in terms of the ideas and attitudes which prevailed in the times in which they were living. Thus, through the study of the teaching of the great Christian thinkers down the centuries it becomes possible to trace the ways in which the main articles of Christian belief were interpreted and understood. Something of the same sort can also be done in relation to our own day and age, and by comparing and contrasting the older interpretations with those of contemporary Christian teaching, we can see how interpretations of beliefs have changed and crystallised down into their present forms. We will again take one or two examples.

In the 3rd century some Christian teachers believed that souls were re-incarnated at death. Before long however, that belief was abandoned and for many centuries now all Christian teachers have maintained that each human soul is a single, unique creation of God. Again, in the early centuries some Christian thinkers produced extremely crude explanations of the way in which God achieved man's redemption. It was taught by some, for instance, that because mankind was in bondage to the Devil through sin, God made a pact with the Devil and promised to surrender to him His Son in exchange for man's freedom. But God cheated the Devil by raising His Son to life again and so won back both mankind from the power of the Devil and His Son from death! Needless to say, such an unworthy interpretation of the Christian doctrine of redemption could not long survive and was abandoned.[1] In the Church of the 11th to the 13th centuries too, other beliefs were current which we now see to have been unsatisfactory. The medieval theologians believed that it was possible to prove by argument the existence of God. In the 16th century the Calvinists, as is well known, stoutly maintained that men were pre-destined by God to eternal life or to eternal damnation. Neither of these convictions finds much currency among Christian thinkers nowadays.

But we need not go so far back as this to find examples of beliefs once firmly maintained by Christians but now discredited. Only one hundred years ago most Christians in this country were being taught that creation was an act accomplished at a definite point in time, that Adam was a single individual, born innocent and perfect, that the serpent in the Genesis story was Satan, and that the Fall was accompanied by the first beginning of sex-relations. In 1860, it is true, there had been published a volume called *Essays and Reviews,* the work of a group of Christian thinkers who held more enlightened views. But it was bitterly attacked as being incompatible with orthodox Christian belief. Moreover, it was in this same year that Samuel Wilberforce, the most eloquent and cultivated of the English bishops of the day, failed abysmally in public debate with T. H. Huxley at Oxford to uphold the literal interpretation of the Genesis account of the creation as against Darwin's evolutionary theories. Thirty years later the now famous volume *Lux Mundi,* edited by Charles Gore, caused a considerable stir in Christian circles by its attempt to reconcile all new knowledge with the Christian revelation. But it marked the beginning of a change, the force of which was irresistible. The essay on *The Christian Doctrine of God* included the following passage:

'We propose to approach the question in the full conviction that the revelation of God in Christ is both true and complete,

---

[1] See J. K. Mozley, *Doctrine of the Atonement,* London, 1915. S. Cave, *The Work of Christ,* London, 1950.

and yet that every new truth which flows in from the side of science, or metaphysics, or the experience of social and political life, is designed in God's providence to make that revelation real, by bringing out its hidden truths. It is in this sense that the Christian revelation of God claims to be both final and progressive; final, for Christians know but one Christ and do not "look for another"; progressive, because Christianity claims each new truth as enriching our knowledge of God, and bringing out into greater clearness and distinctness some half-understood fragment of its own teaching.'[1]

Today the majority of Christian thinkers start from the point of view here expounded and recognise, in consequence, that there is not, nor ever can be, any 'conflict' between science and religion, provided that each observes the limits of the different fields within which it works. An astrophysicist may occasionally still be tempted to say that our modern knowledge of the universe at no point leaves room for the notion of a Creator, but most people recognise at once that in so saying he has ceased to speak as a scientist and is encroaching upon metaphysics, which is outside the terms of reference of his scientific studies. Nowadays, however, scientists are usually careful to keep to their science and theologians to their theology.[2]

We have, in fact, been glancing here at certain aspects of what is technically known as 'Historical Theology'. From this particular branch of theological studies a teacher is able to learn about a collection, as it were, of facts about Christian belief which have clustered, or still cluster around, the basic statements which are contained in the Creeds. And from his study in particular of recent works on Theology, he is able to teach young people how Christians nowadays interpret basic Christian beliefs. Needless to say, he will seldom be able to point to one single interpretation of a particular article in the Creed as being common to all Christians everywhere. But he will be able to indicate in a

---

[1] By Aubrey Moore, p. 58, 6th Edition.
[2] See *Science and Christian Belief*, by C. A. Coulson. Oxford, 1955.

clear and concise manner what are the main interpretations and to explain the differences between them. It would be idle to pretend that the teacher will find this an easy thing to do—not because he here touches upon denominational disagreements, which can be explained fully and sympathetically without any danger of his being or appearing partisan and so offending a basic stipulation of the Education Act — but rather because he must be able to teach plainly and concisely certain facts which have to be culled from what is a living, changing, growing process of experience and thought, and that is never easy. It is basically a simpler matter to teach that the three angles of a triangle together equal 180°, or that Queen Elizabeth I reigned from 1558 to 1603, than it is to teach about the character of Shylock in *The Merchant of Venice* or the artistic approaches of the Florentines or Expressionist painters. So too, it is relatively easy to teach Christian doctrines dogmatically, 'as the bare assertions of an essentially unverifiable authority', rather than 'as the expressions of truths which are capable of being verified — spiritually verified, in some sense, in the experience of all her (the Church's) members; verified intellectually, as well as spiritually, in the reason and experience of her theologians and thinkers and men of learning'.[1] But it is this latter task which the teacher must set himself if his teaching about the facts of Christian belief is to stand any chance of making an impression upon adolescents today. An exacting part of his work, both in preparation and presentation, it will certainly be; yet it can be correspondingly rewarding.

---

[1] A. E. J. Rawlinson — Art: *Authority as a Ground of Belief;* in *Essays Catholic and Critical,* 3rd Edition, p. 96, London, 1929.

CHAPTER 7

RELATING RELIGION TO LIFE

'Unless this withered thing religion . . . ha(s) come alive in our hands, alive and intensely interesting, we may just as well go out and dig the garden until it is time to dig our graves.'

So says Franklin in Shaw's *Back to Methuselah*. His words may well serve as a text for this chapter. They will also speedily correct any false impression which the last chapter may have left in the reader's mind that knowing and teaching the facts about Christianity, important as that is, is an end in itself for religious education. It is, of course, the basis — the only sound basis — upon which the best kind of religious education can be developed. The development must be concerned to show the importance of religion in everyday life.

If it is true that teaching about religion often fails to interest and to create a desire to know more, because it deals too little with basic facts, it can be even more frequently indicted on a charge of failing to relate religion to life. Teachers are aware that this is one of their most difficult tasks and the comments of adolescents themselves frequently suggest that religious teaching seems to them to have little bearing upon life as they see it. Harold Loukes sums up the attitudes of some typical groups of teenagers to religious instruction as follows:

'A few like it as it is, a few want to get rid of it, and the vast majority would like to see more discussion, more give and take, *and a greater relevance to daily life.*'

His conclusion is confirmed by others who have investigated

the attitudes of adolescents to the religious teaching they were given in school.

The suggestion that more discussion lessons would help to bring religion into closer touch with real life is important and is considered at some length below. Clearly, however, it is a teaching method which can be employed fully in the upper rather than the lower part of the secondary school. Meantime, for the more conventional type of lesson the problem has to be tackled in a rather different sort of way. To this we turn first.

Here, above all, the starting-point will be the teacher's own insight into the relevance of the Bible to the everyday life of the children — an insight which is probably the most obvious single result of that study upon the importance of which emphasis has repeatedly been put. This is also the point at which one perceives most plainly the importance of religious teaching being undertaken by the person who is himself religiously minded. If it is true that no one can understand Virgil in the Bucolics unless he has been five years a countryman, or Virgil in the Georgics unless he has been five years a farmer, it is truer still that one must know the religious value of the Bible at first hand before he can bring its teaching to life. So, certainly, Martin Luther, one of the great students of the Bible, found:

> 'Expounding the Scriptures is not like a lawyer's job. . . . No one properly speaks nor hears any Scripture unless he is emotionally in tune therewith, so that he feels within what he hears and speaks without, and says "Aye, truly so it is".'[1]

No doubt the modern teacher who has come to his own religious evaluation of the Bible through a careful study of what the scholars have to say about its origins and nature, finds himself 'emotionally in tune' with it in a somewhat different manner from that which Luther felt — but the principle is basically the same. It must still speak to him of

[1] Quoted *Martin Luther*, by Brian Lunn, London, 1934, pp. 46–7.

'wisdoms old and deep' if he wants the children to catch glimpses of these insights for themselves.

Space allows us to notice, once again, only one or two examples. The Creation-stories in Genesis, for all their pre-scientific mythological framework, stress the belief that the universe is a creation of God and (in chapter 1) man himself the crown of it. This fundamental way of looking at the meaning of life runs, implicitly, or explicitly, through the whole Bible. It is more rather than less important to young people at a time when attention is focussed more on the 'mechanics' of the universe and less on its purpose, and when two world wars and the threat of a third tend to rob the life of the individual of its sense both of dignity and of purpose. Again, the teacher may be less concerned than were his predecessors to teach the details of the history of which the Old Testament is full, but the approach to history which he has found there he will want children to begin to appreciate because it, too, deeply affects a person's whole outlook on human life in general and his own in particular. History can be seen as the sum of human endeavour, achievement and failure, with no frame of reference beyond the human. It can also be viewed, as it is in the Old Testament, in relation to the standards and conduct towards which men must strive in the light of their faith in the existence and character and demands of God. This last attitude to history, which is so prominent a feature of the teaching of the Old Testament prophets and historians, stems from that same sense of a deep, unshakable purpose in human affairs as is reflected in the Creation-stories. With it goes the conviction that ultimately the divine purposes must prevail.[1]

It must not be assumed, of course, that the 'evidence' which the Old Testament prophets and historians drew upon to justify to their contemporaries this view of history will

---

1 Rheinold Niebuhr, the distinguished American theologian, goes so far as to declare: 'The Biblical faith in a divine sovereignty which unifies history remains a permanently necessary basis for the idea of universal history.' (*Faith and History*, London, 1949, p. 127.)

normally carry conviction to adolescents today. Francis Bacon saw, with great insight, that 'Prosperity is the blessing of the Old Testament, adversity is the blessing of the New', and it is the New and not the Old which is here closer to the facts of life. Material prosperity, and success in one form or another — victory in battle, good harvests, good health — are not for the Christian the signs of divine favour and blessing which the Old Testament so often proclaims them to be. From this point of view it is the message of the Cross in the New Testament and not the philosophy underlying, for instance, the Book of Judges in the Old, which gets nearer to the heart of things. Nor is the fondness of the Old Testament historians for 'miraculous' events in Israel's story a reliable guide to young people today who want to know why they should believe that there is a 'divine dimension' to history. These are aspects of that older and cruder form of the belief in God's government of the world which have been dissolved away by 'the acids of modernity'. The Psalmist could declare, out of the very obstinacy of his faith, that he had never seen the righteous forsaken nor his seed begging their bread. But the hollowness of his claim was exposed even by more realistic poets among his compatriots, not least by the author of the Book of Job, and somewhat caustically by a modern poet:

> I have been young, and now am not too old;
> And I have seen the righteous forsaken,
> His health, his honour and his quality taken,
> This is not what we were formerly told.[1]

But if the teacher must therefore be careful to help young people to separate out the wheat from the chaff, as it were, in the Old Testament view of the meaning of history, he must, as Niebuhr is at pains to remind us, be just as anxious to avoid trying to justify the Biblical view of history in terms of one or other of the modern 'secular' theories about the meaning of history. There is a paradox at the centre of the

---

[1] Edmund Blunden — *Report on Experience.*

Biblical view of history which must not be forgotten or explained away. The meaning of history, it declares, is only partly to be seen from within our limited view of it; its ultimate end, and therefore its full meaning, lie beyond the limited vision of the human mind. The prophets return to this fact again and again, but none more insistently than Second-Isaiah:

> Behold, the nations are as a drop of a bucket, and are counted as the small dust of the balance. . . . All the nations are as nothing before him; they are counted to him less than nothing, and vanity.
> My thoughts are not your thoughts, neither are your ways my ways, saith the Lord.
> For as the heavens are higher than the earth, so are my ways higher than your ways, and my thoughts than your thoughts.
> Shall the clay say to him that fashioneth it, What makest thou?[1]

The Apocalyptists too, understood this as they exhorted their countrymen to look beyond contemporary events to the future in order to see their sufferings in full perspective. The author of the Book of Job affirmed it in relation to the explanation of suffering in the life of the righteous man. Jesus accepted it when he embraced the cross in the faith that it was part of the divine purpose. Paul clings to it courageously when he declares:

> All things work together for good to them that love God.
> — and
> Neither death, nor life, nor angels, nor principalities, nor things present, nor things to come, nor powers, nor height, nor depth, nor any other creature, shall be able to separate us from the love of God, which is in Christ Jesus our Lord.

Needless to say, this insistence in the Bible that the full understanding of history lies beyond both time and also the limits of human perception, does not make one wit less important the work and the aims of the secular historian.

[1] Is. 40.15,17; 55.8,9; 45.9.

But it does warn that the most penetrating analysis of the historian, valuable and important as it is up to a point, is bound to be incomplete. 'Bound as our lives are to the tyranny of time, it is through what we know of history that we are delivered from our bonds and escape — into time.'[1] Precisely! — 'escape into time' is what the human perspective of history can offer us. The Bible view of history, as one would hope and expect, is a reminder that for the full meaning of history, whether of societies, or peoples, or individuals, man must 'escape' through faith beyond time into eternity.

> 'There are provisional meanings in history, capable of being recognised and fulfilled by individuals and cultures; but mankind will continue to "see through a glass darkly", and the final meaning can only be anticipated by faith. It awaits a completion when "we shall know even as we are known".'[2]

Could the Bible be more relevant to life than this? Von Schlegel once said that 'A historian is a prophet in reverse', and many teachers can remember being taught that history itself uncovered a story of human progress— from lower to higher and more enlightened modes of life. Adolescents today are without such comforting assurances as they mark the lack of humanity and at times, the savagery, which have characterised recent history. History's 'escape into time' has only partial encouragement to give them. They need, much more than their fathers did, the Bible's reminder that history makes sense of life only with the help of that faith which gives it a 'divine dimension'.

Is it necessary to add that, though the teacher must have thought his way through to something like this depth in his philosophy of history, he will seldom be demonstrating the relevance of the Bible view of history to life in terms of a philosophy of history as such? Most often he will be drawing upon it to illuminate particular problems which trouble

---

[1] A. L. Rowse — *The Use of History,* London, 1946, p. 30.
[2] Neibuhr, Op. cit., p. 243.

adolescents. A girl in her fourth year says with some bitterness:

'During the war when people prayed God couldn't save — he couldn't stop people sending aeroplanes and dropping bombs.'

In contrast, another girl of the same age group has begun to see the point of the Biblical view:

'If someone is very ill but has great faith in God, they expect that God will look after them and guard them and they will make a complete recovery, through God's love for them, and when this seems as if it will happen, and the person begins to get better, everybody . . . begins rejoicing and thanking God. But suddenly she has a relapse and begins to get worse and nothing can be done for her. Perhaps she is given only a few months to live. Then we think that God is being cruel. He gives us our life and takes it away from us. This incident makes us lose faith in God and have a bitter feeling towards him, but this is not really the case, it arises only from the fact that we do not understand.'

So too, has a fifth-year girl:

I think that God tries to guide men, and give them a chance to do what is right.[1]

It is folly, however, to think that particular adolescent problems like these can be dealt with piecemeal by a teacher. Any gleam of light which he can help young people to shed on them can come only out of his understanding of the larger issue of the Biblical philosophy of history of which they are facets.

Most teachers believe that it is in the teaching of the prophets that the relevance of the Old Testament to everyday life can become most obvious to young people. This is due to the fact that Amos, Micah, Hosea and Isaiah in particular were concerned to stress a principle of religious life which is still accepted without question by all civilised people today,

[1] Quoted from *Religion in Education*. Vol. 27, No. 1, Autumn, 1959,

religious and otherwise — namely, that religion (for those who believe in it) must find expression in mercy and justice. Why is it then, that too often an air of unreality and a consequent feeling of irrelevance, creep into far too many secondary school lessons on the 8th century prophets when such 'live' teaching material is ready to hand? Part of the answer probably is that teachers often fail to make allowance for the fact that the prophets speak in a national and not an individual context. 'Israel', 'Jacob', 'Judah' are those to whom they address their stern and uncompromising calls. But what does the adolescent make of a message addressed to a *nation*? True, he is probably conditioned to thinking that politicians still speak to peoples or even 'blocs'. But to him religion is essentially a private and personal matter. So before the message of the prophets can become really relevant to life as he knows it, the teacher must help him to lift it out of its national, Israelite, into an individual, context. Too often, unfortunately, this is not done, with the result that the fact that the prophets speak directly to the 20th century A.D. as well as to the 8th century B.C. is lost on young people.

Children's understanding of these and other Biblical points of view, with their considerable implications for attitudes to life, and problems and questions which crop up in daily life, does not, of course, come easily or quickly. The best kind of teaching returns to these matters in different contexts and in relation to various issues, time after time and a beginning has to be made in the secondary school with first forms.

One of the best ways of relating the more conventional type of scripture lesson to life is by using a question to provoke thought along the lines which the teacher thinks desirable. Two or three fairly obvious examples from actual lessons will indicate the technique more precisely.

(1) A lesson was taken with a 1st year secondary class on the story of the baptism of Jesus. After discussion of the details of the story, the teacher asked, in connection with the reference to the 'heavenly voice', 'Do you think that God

"speaks" to people today?' There followed suggestions by the class — 'Yes, through conscience, through thoughts (in praying), through a preacher, through the Bible.' The teacher added the suggestion that sometimes God also speaks through our friends. This discussion lasted about seven minutes altogether and the class then got down to some written work on the story.

(2) A lesson with a 2nd year secondary class was on the early Christian martyrs. The teacher put the question, 'Do Christians today ever have to face suffering like these early Christians did?' The class produced a number of suggestions — missionaries, German Christians under Hitler, Christian leaders in Communist countries.

(3) In another lesson on Amos, also with a 2nd year secondary class, stress had been put on the prophet's fearlessness in speaking out God's message, especially in face of the threat to his life and liberty made by Amaziah. The teacher asked — 'Can you think of any Christian teachers or leaders in recent years who persisted in speaking out in God's name in spite of attempts to silence them?' This was a fairly searching question but teacher and class between them thought of Pastor Niemöller, Trevor Huddleston, and Roman Catholic Bishops in central Europe.

On other occasions the teacher will provide information which is additional to that actually found in the Bible story and quite deliberately show how it may help to explain what lies behind an incident or Biblical point of view. One very important task of this sort is the attempt to show how the relevance of the Bible message has survived changes in the attitude to the world and human life which provided the framework of that message in earlier, pre-scientific times. The Creation-stories are explained briefly in terms of their Mesopotamian background; some of the 'miracles' of the Old Testament, such as the water from the rock, or the provision of manna and quails, are shown to be explicable, as to the actual occurrence, in terms of natural phenomena. Immoral and sub-Christian standards of conduct in the Old

Testament are set frankly in the social and religious context of earlier Hebrew thought and customs.

As a result of this kind of teaching there is, of course, some 'loss' in the child's mind of the sense of authority and inspiration of the Old Testament in the cruder sense. But this is more than compensated for by the positive gain — the realisation on the part of the child that the Old Testament moves in a world which can be understood in terms of modern thought and is not a collection of fantastic stories about a fairy-tale religious world which strains the credulity of all but the very young, or the un-thinking believer.

There are, of course, other and simpler applications of this same explanatory approach. In the parable of the Lost Coin, for example, a great deal of light is shed upon the woman's frantic search by the possibility that the 'coin' was one section of the precious dowry-necklace which Jewish women wore. The three temptations of Jesus in the wilderness take on an obvious and even striking significance if they are seen as temptations to fall in with three currently accepted beliefs about the Messiah. The theological meaning of the phrase 'eternal life' in the Gospel and Epistles of St. John — a quality of life which begins with the following of Christ in this life and is unchanged by physical death — often comes to older secondary school pupils as a minor revolution in their ideas about the Bible view of 'heaven'.

The most obvious opportunities for showing young people the relevance to life of the New Testament, however, occur in connection with lessons which deal with the *teaching* of Christ and St. Paul. In most Agreed Syllabuses, and with good reason, courses of this particular kind are regarded as appropriate for secondary 3rd to 6th year classes, so that what follows should be read in conjunction with the remarks below about discussion-lesson techniques. It cannot be too strongly emphasised that, contrary to the usual opinion, the teaching of Christ is not always obviously and easily applied to life. Dr. T. W. Manson has declared:

'While the religion of Jesus is undeniably simple, it is not therefore to be regarded as easy of comprehension.'[1]

This is true both of the parables and of the straightforward sayings to be found in the Gospels. Perhaps the main reason for this is that Christ's teaching belongs immediately to a 1st century Palestinian setting, some of which was vastly different from life in 20th century England. To take the sayings first. — 'Let your light so shine before men' — 'Seek ye first the kingdom of God and his righteousness' — 'Blessed are the poor in spirit' — and many others besides do not by any means carry a meaning which is immediately apparent. The Parables present their own kind of difficulty. As stories they are frequently attractive and easily remembered. But when it comes to their meaning, difficulties quickly arise for adults, let alone for adolescents. Dr. Oesterley has said:

> 'Simple as most of the parables seem to be and easy to understand, when first read, there are many which are seen to be very difficult as soon as they are pondered over.'[2]

Some, like the Labourers in the Vineyard, or the Unrighteous Steward, have always been recognised as difficult to interpret. Others carry a message which is by no means obvious — like Dives and Lazarus, or the Wedding Feast. Others again, cannot be fully appreciated without some knowledge of 1st century Palestinian life and customs — the Good Samaritan or the Lost Coin. Finally, there is the difficulty for young people of grasping the idea of a spiritual 'kingdom of heaven' — an easier idea to the Jew of the 1st century A.D. but not one which is part of the normal thought of people today— different aspects of which are referred to in the group of Parables which include the Mustard Seed, the Leaven, the Hidden Treasure, the Pearl of Great Price and the Draw-Net.

For the teacher, of course, most of these difficulties can

[1] *The Teaching of Jesus*, 2nd Edition, London, 1935, pp. 16–17.
[2] *The Gospel Parables*, London, 1936, p. 13.

be overcome by careful reading and study — yet another reminder of the importance of the teacher's own academic preparation. The fact of such difficulties needs to be stressed, however, in order to make it clear that the teacher who embarks on the teaching of the Gospels badly-read and ill-prepared himself, must expect very quickly to find himself confronted by them.

A further obstacle has still to be overcome if a teacher, reasonably secure in his own understanding of the Gospels, is to succeed in helping adolescents to see the relevance of Christ's teaching to their lives in the 20th century. Jesus stressed general principles of the Christian life and not their application to particular circumstances. Indeed, there are indications that he deliberately avoided being led into situations in which he would be legislating on specific issues, such as the question of the permissibility of divorce or the rights and wrongs of paying tribute to Rome. Young people must be helped both to perceive the broad principles which Jesus laid down and also their bearing upon the particular questions and problems which occupy the forefront of their thinking. The principle of concern for one's 'neighbour' can be seen readily enough in relation to the 1st century Palestinian question of Jewish-Samaritan enmity. Adolescents today will also need to be reminded that it has a bearing upon black-white relations in Birmingham or Notting Hill, in the U.S.A., in Kenya or the Republic of South Africa, and upon Arab-Jewish relations in the Middle East. Again, the principle 'Thou shalt love thy neighbour as thyself' must be shown to have a direct bearing upon such matters as the relations between parents and children, between the sexes before and after marriage, between employers and employed, and upon the responsibilities of politicians towards their countrymen — and numerous other present-day issues. Nor is this task made easier for the teacher by the fact that Christians are not always agreed about their attitudes on some of these questions. Dogmatic teaching is inappropriate in any case in lessons on topics of this sort with young people who have to be encouraged to think things through for themselves, but doubly so in view of the lack of a unified Christian attitude to some of them. This is one, but only one, of the reasons why the discussion-lesson is more suitable here: techniques connected with it need to be considered in some detail.

Educational theory long ago abandoned the notion, bequeathed to it by John Locke, that the child's mind is like an empty exercise book, on to which will be inscribed the facts and ideas communicated to the child by the teacher. Instead, teaching has come to be understood in terms of assisting growth or encouraging development. So the best teacher, in the primary as well as the secondary school, tries to know the children he or she teaches — to find out what help this one or that one needs in the complicated business of growing up, not merely in an intellectual but also in an emotional and physical sense and as a social being. Finding out what children themselves think and feel about the things which are learned about in the class-room is therefore an important element in the best teaching at all levels. But plainly, the more the individuality of a child develops, as adolescence advances, the more important it becomes that the learning-process should take into account the attitudes, ideas and feelings of young people. This is vital when a teacher is dealing with religion, which touches the profoundest issues of all. Added to this is the fact which has already been referred to, that the opportunity to discuss the meaning and implications of religious ideas and beliefs is welcomed by young people themselves.

If it be granted then, that certainly from the secondary 4th year upwards, discussion will play a larger part in the teaching of religion than hitherto, the teacher will need to be alive to the pitfalls as well as the advantages which are inherent in this type of lesson. To be profitable, the discussion must be based on an accurate knowledge of those basic facts which are relevant to the topic under consideration. Whether the teacher chooses to furnish them himself, or encourages members of the group to look them up and produce them for the whole group, he must always have them well in mind himself. Nothing is more inimical to useful and purposive discussion than expressions of personal opinion in place of verifiable facts. On the other hand, experienced teachers also know that young people usually have to be encouraged to find out the facts: if allowed to do so, they will more often happily skip this important preparation and embark on a 'discussion' without it.

The teacher has also to devise his own technique for preventing the more vocal members of a group from holding the floor to the exclusion of those who are too shy (or too lazy!) to make a contribution. He has, too, to discover by experience when to intervene himself in order to give an important point emphasis, or to prevent the group from wandering too far from the main point. The teacher who knows his group will be the best judge of how to deal with these dangers.

It should also be remembered that though in discussion the members of a group will teach one another, it will in the main be the teacher's job, as leader of the group, to see that the various ideas, attitudes and opinions which find expression during the discussion are, at various suitable points, or at the end, set squarely against (in this case) the basic Christian principle which is involved or the main views which Christians have come to hold about the matter being considered. Rarely, if ever, can he expect to gain general acceptance for the Christian principle or points of view. But this is not his aim; rather he is concerned to confront young people with the Christian standpoint and to try to ensure that at least they know what it is and why they accept or reject it.

The choice of topics is perhaps the real key to success or failure in the discussion-lesson, and no hard and fast rule can be laid down about this. If a teacher has the respect and confidence of a group they will be ready to suggest topics which they would like to discuss. Most teachers, however, find that though this is a help in planning the discussions, there are topics which they themselves want to add to the list because they are important (though possibly of less conscious concern) to young people at a particular stage. Here the teacher will have to give a good deal of thought to ways and means of 'dressing up' a topic to make it look interesting and relevant. To include in the list of subjects for the term's work topics such as 'Is the Bible inspired?' or 'The Christian view of marriage' would be less likely to stimulate interest than those with a less obviously theological and more practical appeal — 'Is the Bible old-fashioned?' or 'Sex and Marriage'.

Almost as important as the choice of interesting topics is the discovery of varied and interesting ways of introducing them. Real-life events, comment and opinions, drawn from radio, T.V., the cinema, newspapers, magazines and books which form part of the everyday world inhabited by young people (rather than the teacher's world, and certainly not his heavier reading in history or theology) offer the best source-material. Teachers who want more detailed examples of lessons worked out along these lines will find suggestions in *Teenage Religion*[1]. The author's comments about the effort required from the teacher if he is to conduct lessons of this kind successfully are worth quoting:

'The rôle of the teacher in this approach is far more exacting than that he is accustomed to fill. Instead of being an exponent, in direct control of the situation, he becomes a contributor exercising the gentlest of control by the most indirect means. Instead of working outwards from a text or prepared scheme, he works inwards from novel and un-systematic situations. Instead of netting his fish he must tickle them and hope that they will swim in the right direction.'[2]

[1] pp. 116–144.　　　　　[2] p. 149.

CHAPTER 8

AGREED SYLLABUSES

THE Education Act of 1944 did not, of course, create the Agreed Syllabuses; it merely set upon their use the stamp of official approval. Yet it is no exaggeration to say that the provisions for religious education which were eventually incorporated in the Act were to a very great extent made possible by the fact that these Syllabuses had, during the preceding fifteen years or so, won widespread approval and had become widely used.

The Syllabuses were the work of groups of teachers, clergy and ministers, and representatives of the Local Education Authorities and reflected the agreements which existed between Anglican and Free Church people. Thus the Syllabuses could form the basis of religious teaching in the schools in which denominational teaching was inappropriate. The first Syllabus, that of the West Riding of Yorkshire, appeared as has been said, in 1923 and was followed a year later by the first Cambridgeshire Syllabus. Others appeared in succeeding years and the 1944 Act required every Local Education Authority to authorise one for use in the schools under its direction. Some Authorities produced new Syllabuses; others adopted or adapted one of those already in use. When the last complete survey was done (1953) it was discovered that:

In 49 County Education Authorities, 22 had their own Syllabus,

26 used that of another Authority,
1 still used a pre-War (1914) Syllabus

In 79 County Boroughs,   28 had their own,

51 used that of another Authority.[1]

Before 1944 the Cambridgeshire Syllabus was very widely used. Since 1944 it would appear that it has come to share this distinction with the Sunderland Syllabus and that next in order of popularity come those of Surrey, the West Riding, and Durham.

The 1944 Act laid down the procedure which was to be followed in order to produce (or revise) an Agreed Syllabus. It empowered the Local Education Authorities to set up a 'Standing Advisory Council on Religious Education', the function of which is to advise the Authority on matters connected with the religious instruction to be given in accordance with an Agreed Syllabus, and in particular, as to methods of teaching, choice of books, and the provision of lectures for teachers. Such Councils are made up of the representatives of the Local Education Authority, of the Church of England, of the Free Churches, and of the teachers. Some of the most recent revisions of Syllabuses to be made are the Bristol and the Warwickshire (both 1960) and others are at present nearing completion in the counties of Kent and Surrey.

The fact that in every area of England and almost every part of Wales[2] an Agreed Syllabus of Religious Instruction is available for use in county schools is in happy contrast to the situation which prevailed in the first twenty years of this century. Then, the progress of religious education was hampered as we have seen, by denominational arguments; but after 1920 attention was increasingly focused upon the large measure of agreement which exists between the Church of England and the Free Churches as to belief and worship

---

[1] Figures quoted from *Religious Education in Schools*, London, 1954.

[2] *The Welsh Syllabus*, issued in 1945, by the Welsh Society of the Institute of Christian Education, was adopted by all but two of the Welsh L.E.A.'s for use in their schools. A revised syllabus was prepared in 1962.

and their concern that this should form the basis of religious teaching in the schools. Thus the appearance of the Agreed Syllabuses marked a most important step forward in religious education and this fact should be borne in mind in connection with such criticisms as are here made of the existing Syllabuses.

Inevitably perhaps, there were some (and still are a few) who felt that Christian teaching which is not closely geared to the teaching and worship of a specifiic Church was bound to fall short of the ideal. There has thus been some criticism of what was most unjustly called 'Agreed Syllabus Christianity', with the implication that it amounted to a 'watered down' version of the real thing. It is difficult to be patient about this kind of criticism, for it is both wrong in fact, so far as the character of the teaching is concerned, and also quite impracticable. Either it is suggesting that one particular type of Church teaching be given to all the children in the schools, in which case the other major denominations should be given the same right and the schools become denominational recruiting-grounds, or it is implying that no Christian teaching at all should be given in the schools, a position which would be unsatisfactory from an educational, and lamentable from the Christian, point of view.

The fact is that the teaching which is possible through the use of an Agreed Syllabus can encompass, as we have seen, not only the Bible and the story of Christianity, but also the beliefs which are expressed in the two great Creeds of the Churches — the Apostles' and the Nicene. Such teaching, together with the regular daily worship in the School Assembly, provide the opportunity to lay a solid foundation of interest in and understanding of the Christian faith and way of life. On that foundation the Churches can build, and build all the more effectively, if only they can attract young people into their congregations and keep their loyalty and affection. Some of the Syllabuses themselves suggest that the religious education given in the schools should be the means of leading children towards membership of some such worshipping community (For example, the Sunderland, Derbyshire, Lindsey and East Riding Syllabuses). Whether or not this be the outcome with individual children will obviously depend on other factors besides the work and influence of the school, and, in the last resort, as much upon the child's home and local church as the school. Heads and teachers of religion in schools often do what they can to build up the friendliest of relationships between their school and the local clergy and ministers.[1]

Teachers who engage in the work of religious education in schools are certainly under no illusions about the fact that the religious education which they help to provide can never be an end in itself: they are not working towards a 'school religion' or 'Churchless Christianity'. On the other hand, they are equally clear about the fact that *as teachers* it is no part of their task to help fill the pews in the Churches. That is the task of the Churches themselves. The correct appreciation of the relationship between the work of the schools in religious education and the Churches is to see them as complementary to one another — not as alternatives. The occasional critic of 'Agreed Syllabus religion' might well reflect upon the fact that teaching religion in schools is today a 'frontier activity'. That is to say, to try to stimulate interest in religious faith and values among *all* the youngsters in a school, often without any positive home influence to fall back on, and in an age when materialistic pre-occupations over-shadow almost everything else in many people's attitudes to life, does indeed make the teaching of religion one of the most exacting tasks which any educationist today is called upon to tackle. It is encouraging to know that the vast majority of clergy and ministers are well aware of this and

[1] A recent report of the Institute of Christian Education has drawn attention to the need for 'more local efforts in co-operation and partnership to be made by men and women who see the leading and building into the local worshipping community of the instructed and challenged boy and girl as an essential priority in the present field of Christian Education.' (*Partnership in Christian Education*, 1962, p. 44.)

are ready to give teachers all the support and encouragement that they can.

The Agreed Syllabuses also have their critics among the teachers themselves. The commonest complaints here are about the unsuitability of some of the material suggested for lesson topics, of the lack of guidance supplied to the teacher who is not a specialist in theology or Biblical studies, and that the Syllabuses are often too 'pietistic' and 'other-worldly' in their whole approach. There is some force in all these criticisms. It has been widely recognised in recent years that though some Syllabuses do suggest alternative schemes of work for less-able groups, on the whole they are geared more closely to the interests, and general approach to teaching, of the grammar school. Most of them take it for granted that a basically historical and literary approach to the Old Testament and the New, to the story of the Church, and even to questions of conduct and worship, is the right one for the secondary school pupil.

For a large number in the secondary modern groups, and even for some in the grammar schools, a much more helpful approach would be that which begins with actual situations, or everyday facts and existing institutions. Here, it is argued, a teacher has a real point of contact with the realised experience of these youngsters, who want to see more of what religion is actually doing and what it means in the life they are living, than of its origins and history and literature. It will be evident from what was said in the two preceding chapters that to recognise the force of this argument is not to suggest for a moment that the teacher of less-able groups is to be encouraged to think that he can avoid the task of teaching such youngsters the basic facts about Christianity. Nor will it be thought to imply that the historical-literary approach to religious teaching *need* be any the less relevant to actual life-situations: it has been emphasised again and again throughout this book that it can be made extremely relevant, if the teacher is concerned that it be so. The point at issue is the more practical one of how best to arouse interest and establish a point of contact. Many teachers believe that, as has been said, for the less-able child, interest can be aroused by starting from existing facts, events, situations and institutions with which young people are familiar, and then gradually working back to the presentation of the historical and Biblical data which are essential for an adequate understanding of the Christian faith and way of life.

One or two examples may help to make clearer what is envisaged by this difference of approach. A number of Syllabuses suggest that in the secondary school a course should be provided on the Apostolic Church, and provide a list of passages from the Acts of the Apostles and the New Testament Epistles upon which such a course of lessons could be based. For the child whose interests are not primarily historical and literary a better plan would be to begin with the facts about the worship and other activities of the local Churches to which some members of the class will belong, and the structure and furnishings of the buildings where the congregations worship in the neighbourhood where the children live. They could be taken into the churches themselves and be given a talk by the clergy and ministers about the uses to which the various objects in the church are put and about the societies, clubs and other gatherings which meet during the week as part of the other activities of the Church. Out of such visits would come questions about the furnishings, the services and the other activities of the congregation. Lessons in school would deal with these matters by touching upon facts about the Church in the New Testament and about the Churches in their later history. The facts and the beliefs thus studied would assume real significance because they explained matters in which these youngsters' interest would have been aroused.

Again, a short course of lessons on the general theme of Christ's work as healer of the sick need not always begin with the conventional study of the relevant New Testament narratives which is suggested in most Syllabuses. A film like *The Nun's Story*, which is concerned with the work and experiences of a member of a Community which makes itself responsible for (among other things) medical work in the Congo, could be used as the starting-point for questions and discussion which would lead back to facts about Christ's concern for the sick. It could also be made to raise important and valuable questions about the New Testament itself, about prayers for the sick, and about 'miracles', all of which would gain in interest because the film would have provided a vivid point of contact with the everyday world of the youngsters. Stories (well-told, which keep to the facts and are devoid of pious adornments or sentimental implications) about outstanding people and their achievements, taken from various walks of life, can be made to provide a similarly stimulating introduction to other aspects of the life and work of Christ and the Church in the Gospels and Epistles.

It is of prime importance to recognise that this kind of indirect approach to the teaching of religion places a very heavy load on the teacher. His aim must be quite clear — to lead back from interesting, day-to-day material towards the discovery of essential facts and principles in the Bible and later Church history or facts about Christian doctrine. It is all too easy to stop short with the interesting facts, story, film, T.V. item or book, and to fail to connect it, skilfully and without too evident a drop in the level of interest, with the basic facts of the Christian faith and life of which the less-able child needs to be just as much aware as his intellectually abler contemporaries. The teacher needs to be more, rather than less, sure of his ground as well as more imaginative and skilful in planning his lessons. In some ways it demands less imagination and ingenuity to start with a passage from the Bible and go on from there, than it does to follow the lines here suggested. All, therefore, that has been said in earlier chapters about the need for the teacher to have read and studied and thought about theology and Biblical studies applies just as surely to the teacher of less-able children as it does to his colleague working with groups of greater intellectual ability.

This last point also has some bearing upon the second criticism which we noted above, that the Syllabuses pre-suppose too much academic knowledge and information on the part of the teachers. They do, and they must, pre-suppose this kind of knowledge! There is no short-circuiting of this fact, as has been made plain in earlier pages. The Syllabuses are guides, not prescribed outlines of work ready-made to be produced for classes just as they stand. The more knowledge and insight the teacher brings to the working out of the suggestions contained in the Syllabus, the better his lessons are bound to be. Conversely, the less he has read and studied and thought, the more difficult is he bound to find a Syllabus to use as the basis of good religious teaching.

This is a 'hard saying' and one from which those who write about the teaching of religion sometimes shy away; yet it is confirmed over and over again in the experience of teachers themselves and has to faced frankly. The Sheffield Report, to which reference was made earlier, comes to the conclusion that for many non-specialist teachers the Agreed Syllabus becomes itself a scheme of work which they try to cover at all costs, rather than a general guide with the help of which a scheme of work is drawn up for a particular school.[1] The report appears to imply that this points to a defect in the Syllabuses and there is no doubt that many of them are sometimes rather too ambitious as to the type and quantity of teaching which they assume can be given in two periods (let alone one) a week per class. These difficulties could be largely overcome however, if every secondary school had on its staff at least one teacher who had made some specialised study of divinity. He can draw up a practicable scheme of work for the school, with the general guidance of the Syllabus, and give some guidance to the non-specialists who will be sharing the teaching of religious knowledge with him. If this is not done, and if the non-specialists are merely given the Agreed Syllabus to work from as they will, then the

[1] Op. cit., p. 47.

Syllabus itself will usually become, as the report says, a scheme of work, with the most unsatisfactory results.

The third criticism to which reference was made may be elaborated in the words of this same report:

> 'Agreed Syllabuses (are) too "idealistic" in their approach. Their compilers (appear) to have been afraid that too historical an approach might obscure the doctrine, and as a result (tend) to the other extreme, even become pietistic and "other-worldly" in emphasis.'[1]

Some teachers might prefer to use the word 'theological' rather than 'idealistic' but the main issue is the same and represents fair criticism of the general standpoint from which the material has been arranged in some Syllabuses. Even some of the most recent of the revisions appear to suffer from this same weakness. Theology is, needless to say, important: indeed, it is, as was earlier stressed, impossible for a teacher to teach the Old and New Testaments adequately without frequent use of, and reference back to, his own insights into Christian doctrine. But the theology should be allowed to emerge naturally out of the appropriate sections of the Bible as they come to be understood in their historical setting. All teachers, but especially non-specialist teachers, would find the Syllabuses easier to use as bases for particular schemes of work if the sections of the Bible used in them were chosen and arranged on this principle rather than on the basis of some abstruse, over-all Christian theological theme — whether it be derived from what is nowadays often referred to as 'Biblical Theology', or 'Typology', or what we will.[2] The Sheffield Report is fully

---

[1] pp. 14–15.

[2] It is the fundamental failing of Christian Biblical theologians — or certainly of some of them — that they . . . impose upon the Old Testament, in a mechanical and uncritical fashion, the categories of traditional Christian dogmatics in order to prove, not merely the historical connection between the two Testaments but also the theological unity of the two, and in doing so treat the Old Testament as a Christian book although it is not and never can be and never should be regarded as such.' P. Wernberg-Möller, in an article in the *Hibbert Journal*, Vol. 59, October, 1960, p. 25.

justified in asking that it be recognised that 'doctrine (is) conveyed most successfully when history (is) allowed to show God's Revelation'.[1] It is much to be hoped that future revisions of Agreed Syllabuses will follow this principle and so render the Syllabuses more readily understandable by the teachers who want to use them.

Finally, we can hardly avoid asking, in connection with the Syllabuses, an even more searching question. When used as imaginatively as their authors hoped that they would be, are they, by and large, the most suitable types of Syllabuses for teaching young people what religion is and can mean to them? The answer of many teachers who have used them over a long period with many groups of children would probably be a qualified affirmative. Their great virtue is that all of them without exception concentrate attention upon the three bases of the Christian tradition and sources of Christian faith, worship and practice, without which young people's understanding of the religion would be woefully inadequate. These bases are — the Bible, the perennial spring of living Christian experience; Christian beliefs, crystallized out of the Church's actual living-out of that experience; and finally, some glimpses of the story of the Church itself and of the lives of some of her outstanding leaders, saints and teachers. It is surely one of the more notable achievements of their various compilers, that they have been concerned that religious education should develop upon so firm a basis of solid Christian tradition and not be allowed to deteriorate into that kind of vague agglomeration of religious ideas and aspirations which is sometimes referred to as 'the religion of the spirit'. This kind of phrase too often means little more than whatever religious or quasi-religious beliefs, ranging from a vague theism to a spiritualised humanism or a mystical pantheism, happen to appeal to this individual or that.

This is not, for one moment, to decry the value of such

[1] p. 15.

beliefs for the individual who holds to them and lives by them; it ill-becomes any of us to think lightly of the faith and religious experience by which others live and to which they may well have come along a hard road of doubt, perplexity and perhaps some suffering. Nevertheless, individual interpretations of religious faith and experience do not and cannot form a sufficiently solid and reliable basis for teaching young people about religion. They have the right to begin where the broad, main-stream of Christian religious faith and experience begins and to share if they will in a much more solidly grounded and widely tested tradition than the experience of any single individual could ever supply. Even if, in the last resort, there may be some of them who will feel it necessary to forge for themselves a faith and some form of religious experience which depart to some extent from what might be called the 'orthodox' Christian tradition, (and doubtless there will inevitably be some), sound educational principles and sound Christian teaching alike require that they be allowed to do this against the background of an understanding of what the main-stream of Christian belief, faith, worship and practice has to offer them. Nor must the many limitations and short-comings, past as well as present, of orthodox and organised Christianity, be allowed to obscure the fact that for millions orthodox religion has itself proved very much a 'religion of the spirit'. For them, St. Paul's phrase 'the fellowship of the Spirit' has had real significance, as expressing their own experience of the fact that the Spirit works within the whole body of the Church and within the individual as a member of the Church.

It is, however, as we have seen, when it comes to the selection and presentation of the material that some of the Syllabuses need considerable, and most of them at least some, re-thinking and re-planning. In addition to the matters already mentioned, there could well be more time given to, and some extremely interesting material provided for, the learning about the Churches in more recent times, and especially the Churches today, in this country and overseas. Time should be spent on learning about such important developments as the Ecumenical Movement, the Church of South India, the Churches in Germany under the Nazis, Christianity in the U.S.S.R. and similar matters. Interesting and important as is the past history of the Church, it is in the life of the Churches today that some of the young people who are receiving part of their religious education through the schools will play their part and about which they need to know more.[1]

Again, most of the Syllabuses are by no means at their best in dealing with the application of Christian principles to life — individual, social and international. It was remarked earlier that teachers are bound to find this aspect of New Testament teaching difficult. The Syllabuses do little to help them to overcome their difficulties, often having nothing better to offer than somewhat vague summaries of New Testament passages lumped together under a general heading such as 'Personal and Corporate Religion', 'The Christian Life', 'The Teaching of Christ'.

Both of these weaknesses relate, of course, to teaching at secondary level but mention ought also to be made of a fault which concerns the work at the junior stage. It was suggested earlier that the years 9-11 are in many respects the most suitable at which to teach in some detail facts about 'The History of Everyday Things' (to use the title of a well-known series of children's history books) in Israel in Old Testament times, and in Palestine and the northern Mediterranean countries visited by St. Paul, in New Testament times. Without the kind of detailed but interesting teaching about the lives of the people and countries with which the Bible is concerned, the later teaching in the

1 This opinion is apparently shared by the group whose deliberations led to the Sheffield Report. They criticised Agreed Syllabuses because, among other things, 'many (of them) did not deal sufficiently with Christian life and experience in the 20th century. Often the story of the Churches' experience for the last 1900 years (is) handled inadequately.' p. 14.

secondary school lacks much of its freshness and some of its meaning. Secondary school teachers often find a gap here in the knowledge of their 1st forms and feel obliged to try to cover, all too hurriedly, the more important of these facts when they would wish to be able to get ahead with the next stage of the teaching.

If it is granted that these three additions, at least, ought to be made to the Syllabuses, clearly some of the existing material has to go to make room for them. There are two points at which useful pruning could be done. There is still too much attention given to less-important parts of the Old Testament history. The history of Israel should certainly be known in general outline by the time a child reaches the 3rd secondary year, because it provides the necesssary background for the teaching about permanently valuable religious ideas of the Old Testament which can begin to be examined at this stage. Moreover, since Israel's faith was rooted in the conviction that God revealed himself primarily in Israel's history, a knowledge of the main outlines of that history are obviously essential for an appreciation of what this faith amounted to. But neither of these requirements can be held to justify the amount of time which it is suggested be spent on the details of some of the historical sections of the Old Testament. It is true that we no longer teach lists of the kings of Judah and Israel but we are still encouraged to spend too much time on the patriarchal stories (already known as stories from junior school days), the invasion of Canaan, the Judges, and the period of the monarchy.

Again, in some Syllabuses valuable time is spent studying two, or all three of the Synoptic Gospels in detail in successive years. Bearing in mind the fact that St. Mark is largely to be found in the Gospels of Matthew and Luke — and sometimes reproduced there in identical language — there is a clear case for pruning at this point too.

No doubt some teachers will feel that even these fairly substantial suggestions for improving the content of the Syllabuses do not go quite far enough. They feel that a strong case could be made out for introducing into the teaching from 3rd secondary year upwards more material from contemporary literature, art and music in particular. They point to the fact that religion expresses itself in many different human interests and activities and that to introduce young people to such wider expressions of religious experience can be stimulating in itself and also help to underline the fact that religion is concerned, or should be, with all that is best in human life and experiences. With this argument many will feel the greatest sympathy. Indeed, it is worth pointing out that at least one recent Syllabus (Hertfordshire 1954) goes some way towards encouraging just this kind of approach to the teaching of religion with older pupils. The practical difficulty about introducing into the Syllabuses explicit outlines of courses which use this kind of material, is that of selecting from a very wide area just the material which would command general approval. Obviously what is chosen will depend, to a very large extent, upon the interests of the individual teacher. Certainly the freedom which the Syllabuses already give to the teachers to select and adapt their material in the way which seems to them best, would fully justify any teacher who so desired in introducing contemporary material at any points at which it seemed desirable to do so.

It seems advisable to end this discussion of the Agreed Syllabuses by re-iterating the point that such criticisms of them as it has been necessary to make have been put forward out of a desire that the Syllabuses should be made more effective and come to be even more widely used. Criticism of them should not be allowed to obscure the fact that, even as they stand, they represent a tremendous advance in religious education and have already helped to transform religious teaching in the schools. They have now been used fairly widely and for long enough to enable some of their defects as bases for effective schemes of work to become apparent. The best tribute that can be paid to the vision, imagination and courage of their various authors, would be to ensure that they are made, as speedily as may be, still more effective. Conversely, to allow them to be increasingly disregarded and eventually cast aside for want of honest criticism and consequent revision would be to risk losing the valuable ground which, through them, their authors helped to gain for the cause of religious education in the schools.

CHAPTER 9

SCHEMES OF WORK

FROM all that has been said in the last chapter certain practical implications stand out. The teacher who wants to make the teaching of religion effective in his school must not use the Agreed Syllabus as if it were itself a scheme of work but use it to guide him in drawing up his own scheme. Furthermore, it will be apparent that in doing this he will most certainly want to make a selection of the teaching material, Biblical and other, which he is to use in his lessons, and/or to use it sometimes in a different manner from that suggested in the Syllabus.

Many teachers need to be assured that they are in fact free to do this and a glance at the Introductions to most Syllabuses will convince them on this point. Most Syllabuses go out of their way not only to allow, but to encourage, the teacher who is using the Syllabus to use it in just this sort of way. Thus the London Syllabus (1947) says:

> 'It cannot be overstressed that the Syllabus is planned to be suggestive rather than compulsory, and that a slavish adherence to, or a blind following of, the contents in their entirety will defeat its own ends, and be contrary to the spirit in which the Syllabus has been written.' (p. 29)

The Middlesex (1948) says:

> 'It cannot be too strongly affirmed that the desire of the Drafting Committees is to leave as much freedom as possible to the teachers.' (p. 7)

The Cambridgeshire (1949) insists that:

113

'The object of the Syllabus is to serve as a guide and not as a hard and fast scheme of actual lessons.' (p. 16)

The effectiveness of a scheme of work will depend in the first place upon the clarity and suitability of the aims which the teacher has in mind in planning the work at various levels. Two considerations have here to be balanced one against the other and brought into a workable synthesis. On the one hand the teacher is aware of the themes and topics which, because of their intrinsic importance for the child's understanding of and (he hopes) interest in religion, need to find a place in the scheme of work. On the other, he has to bear in mind the levels of ability, experience and interest which particular groups of children will normally have attained at the various stages of their school life and try to ensure that his choice of themes and topics, together with the manner of presenting them to the children, will be within the appropriate range — stimulating enough to develop their interest and activity without at the same time going too far beyond their powers or range of experience.

His problem here is no different from that which confronts the teacher who is planning schemes of work for other parts of the curriculum: the need for such planning is the more easily obscured in his case, however, by the fact that his main 'text-book', the Bible, is more often looked at, as was pointed out in the last chapter, theologically rather than as source-material for the education of the young.[1]

Up to about the age of 7 the religious education of the child will be going on not through 'instruction' so much as through his experiences of and with adults — particularly those, like the parents, and later the teacher, who stand in a close relationship to him. The sense of security and affection which they are able to give him, together with the influence upon him of their own behaviour and attitudes

---

[1] Some of the better text-books now available for use in connection with religious education in schools are helpful here, though the teacher must be on his guard against others which tend to ignore the need for grading Biblical and other material. See Bibliography for details.

towards him and others with whom he and they are associated, are the main means by which the very young child begins to experience those feelings and to develop those attitudes and habits which will later come to be more specifically associated with religious beliefs and practice. His feelings also about the world of nature, about cherished possessions, his early enjoyment of music and dance, of words, colour and music, all these can serve to develop feelings and attitudes which will later become important for his ability to move on into maturer forms of religious experience. Therefore all these things should enter, as fully as possible, into the activities of the infant school and be regarded by the teacher as aspects of the religious education of the very young child, just as surely as they are part of his education in a wider sense as well.

The aims of religious education at the junior school stage were discussed in outline in chapter 4. It was there suggested that the most appropriate teaching material for the child of from 7-11 years is that which focuses attention upon people and their activities. The scheme of work in religious education will be such as will help to familiarise the child with some of the best-known and most-loved stories about people who figure in the Bible, and obviously in this selection stories about Jesus himself will play a large part. There will also be a selection of stories of people from later times who figure prominently in the story of Christianity. (Some would want to include some lessons on great men of other religions, though it might be argued that it would be wiser, on the whole, to defer teaching about these until the secondary stage.)

Obviously it is important that these topics should be chosen with care: the fact that a story is in the Bible is not, in itself, a guarantee that it is edifying teaching material for a child. Some of the Elijah-stories, that about Jephthah's daughter, the story of the proposed sacrifice of Isaac, and those dealing with slaughters in battles, are most unsuitable for the kind of purpose which the teacher will have in mind and should obviously be omitted at this stage. Stories about Jesus should be told or illustrated in a straightforward manner and without the aura of sentimentalism which is still to be seen reflected in some of the printed pictures which are available for use in connection with primary school religious teaching. This last danger will be avoided the more easily if, in the last two years of the primary school course, a good deal of time is given, as was suggested in chapter 4, to the learning about the people and customs of Palestine in Old and New Testament times. For this purpose there is now a wealth of authentic historical data available which can be used both for the teacher's own material and also to guide the children in their drawing and painting of pictures and friezes and in the making of models.[1] The value of this part of the primary course is considerable. Not only will it help to make real and vivid the scenes about which the children have been learning in the stories they have heard or read, and the people whose characters and behaviour they have been unconsciously assimilating: it will also pave the way for the more consecutive work which will fall to be done on the Bible and the story of Christianity in later times, upon which they will be embarking in the first years of the secondary school.

But if selectivity is the hall-mark of the good primary school scheme of work for religious education, so it is also of the secondary school scheme, though with a different end in view. The child of 11-12 years is still more at home with fairly straightforward facts, rather than with more abstract ideas, even if he can now begin to see the chronological connection between people and events. The 1st and 2nd years, then, are the best time at which to begin to draw together the stories from the Old Testament and the New which he has learned in earlier years as stories, and to fill them out with as much further detail as is necessary (and no more) in order to give him an outline picture of the story of Israel, of the life and work of Jesus, and of the beginnings

[1] See Bibliography.

and spread of the Christian Church. It is here that the immense value of the time which he spent in the primary school on learning about the people and customs of Palestine comes into its own. When he hears of the tribes travelling through 'the Wilderness' under Moses, he can the more quickly and easily conjure up the picture of the conditions in which they lived. He will be able to furnish details of what a Palestinian city like Jericho was like, what Samaria was like in the time of Amos, or what the Jewish house was like through the roof of which his friends lowered the paralytic down, and of the 'bed' on which they had carried him there. He will be less likely to confuse Temple with synagogue, or Pharisees with Sadducees, and may even be able to fill in, imaginatively, some of the details of life and customs in non-Palestinian cities of the 1st century which are alluded to in the story of Paul's work in the Acts.

No doubt, as was suggested in chapter 4, abler children in these first two years of the secondary school will themselves raise, or be ready for the teacher to raise, matters which go beyond the acquisition of mainly historical and geographical facts about the history of Israel, the life and work of Jesus, and the story of the Church in earlier and later times. The teacher will welcome the opportunity of introducing them to some of the more difficult ideas and facts which they will be looking at more fully later — the idea of 'progressive revelation', of the 'miraculous' in the Old and New Testaments, of Hebrew ideas about a theocracy, about the ark, or the sacred 'ban' in connection with her mode of fighting, of the prophet as one who was concerned more with his own times than with future events, or with 1st century Jewish ideas about 'evil spirts', heaven and hell, the Law, and so forth. But these will be in the nature of adjuncts to the course — points at which links can begin to be forged with the more advanced teaching which he is to follow in the 3rd-5th (and perhaps 6th) secondary years. The major aim for the teacher in these first two years will be to lay an accurate but vivid foundation of historical and geographical facts and an outline chronology, for the teaching which can be attempted from about age thirteen onwards.

Needless to say, this kind of aim does not ignore the child's immediate religious needs at this stage: they exist and are to be met, so far as the teacher can help to do so, in the classroom as well as in the Assembly and (one may hope) the home. In so far as they can be met by this part of the course it will be from several directions. The child will see that religion concerns real people and real events. In particular, he will be deepening, in a quite concrete fashion, his insights into the religious life as he sees more of the life and work of Jesus, and, after him, that of Paul and, later in the story, that of men like Polycarp, Ambrose, Benedict, Columba, Francis of Assissi, Erasmus, Luther, Francis Xavier, George Fox, John Knox, John Wesley, Charles Kingsley, William Booth, and many others. All these glimpses of religion at work in the lives of men, taught in the right way, can be for the 11-13 year-old a largely unconscious but vastly important deepening of his own religious experience.

From the 3rd secondary year upwards the child's growing vocabulary and deepening of thought and experience makes it possible for the teacher to begin the exceedingly difficult task of teaching about the more important religious ideas, experiences and beliefs which have up till now been glimpsed only briefly. The fact had better be faced frankly that this is the point at which a good deal of religious teaching falls down rather badly. The source-material is mainly (though not entirely) that which has been used earlier — the Old Testament, the New, and the later story of the Church. To the child it looks superficially as if he now goes over 'the Bible' again from which he has been learning for two years already in the secondary school. And, indeed, unless the teacher is quite clear about the distinctive, and to some extent different, aims which are before him for these later secondary years of religious education, the child is, unfortunately, only too likely to be right!

In fact, he should not only be wrong but quickly see that

he is wrong. For he should soon see that not only is he going to use certain parts of the Bible which he has not studied before, but also that even the parts that are superficially familiar to him he is seeing in a new light. All this because he is being paid the compliment of beginning to be treated by his teacher as someone who can learn to think about religion in adult terms. For this is, in sober fact, what the teacher ought to be trying to do now. From now on, he will have as his main aim the task of introducing the child to some of the profoundest religious faith and experience which has emerged in the history of the human race. Israel's conviction that creation itself and human history can reveal, to those who have eyes to see, the presence and purpose of God. The belief of her greater prophets (for which they often suffered) that the truly religious man is the man who cares for justice and compassion and who resists oppression and ruthless self-seeking in the individual and in the community as a whole. Her emergence from lower stages of belief towards the peak conviction that there is but one supreme God of all mankind from whose purpose men can for a time turn aside, but who can bring good out of evil and use even suffering for men's ultimate good. For their fuller understanding of the message of Christ in the New Testament the teacher will try to introduce them to some of the Jewish beliefs which form the context in which Christ's teaching was largely set, or by contrast with which its implications stand out the more clearly. Notions like the 'kingdom of God', the 'Messiah', the Jewish pre-occupation with religion as the keeping of the Law, their worship in Temple and synagogue, their attitude to Gentiles, 'sinners', Samaritans and Romans. It will be by helping them to see how the attitudes and explicit teaching of Christ emerge from, or contrast starkly with, these and other attitudes and beliefs of his contemporaries, that these youngsters will be able to see Christ's message more plainly for what it really is.

But there will be the more perplexing aspects of the teaching to be examined frankly as well. The implications of this teaching for people today; the Parables which, as has been made clear already, are by no means always easy to comprehend; the element of the miraculous in the Gospels, whether in connection with Christ's person (the Virgin Birth, the Resurrection and the Ascension) or his work (especially the nature miracles, the miracles of the raising of the dead.) There will also be the Church's beliefs about Christ himself (his Divinity), the Holy Spirit, the Atonement, to be faced with frankness and with a proper regard for traditional Christian beliefs about such matters.

Some Church History will have to find a place at a similarly deeper level of insight and understanding. The life and perplexities of the early Christians to whom Paul wrote at Corinth and Thessalonica, and the personal but important letter to Philemon, together with the information about early Church life given in the Acts. The condition and life of the Churches in more recent times must also, for the reasons given earlier, find a place in these years' work. Some insights into the work and witness of Christians overseas in the last one hundred and fifty years — Christianity under the Nazis, the Church of South India, the story of the Ecumenical Movement — are perhaps less-well known and somewhat more important for young people today than a more obvious course on the work of the Christian Missions in the 19th century. And, as though all this were not enough to fit in and teach interestingly and thoughtfully, room has to be found, before these youngsters leave school, for short courses about the Bible itself (its origins and the nature of its authority), about Christian beliefs in an age of science, and about the existence of great religions other than Christianity.

It is evident that even with an allowance of two periods a week for religious education, the teacher will have to select with great care the best material from all that is available to put into this part of the scheme of work. This is all to the good, because a series of shorter courses, with limited but stimulating aims behind them, is infinitely more likely to arouse and sustain the interest of the average 13-15 year-old than too lengthy and detailed a course on, say, the Old Testament or the Gospels, or the Acts and the Epistles, or the early history of the Church. What must not be sacrificed, however, at any point, is the degree of interest in the presentation of the topics which are chosen for a particular short course or the intellectual effort which is expected of the pupils. The former point is obvious; the latter less so and the cause of much falling-away of interest in religious education on the part of pupils in the upper part of the secondary school. Every teacher of religion in the secondary school has experienced and had to struggle against the increasing assumption on the part of youngsters from the 3rd form upwards that one can sit back and relax in the religious education lesson! The remedy is in the teacher's hands — to insist, by his own standards of preparation and actual teaching, and by those which he demands in any work that the pupils do for him, that he gets the same attention and careful and exact thought in learning about religion as he or his colleagues insist upon in connection with other class-room activities.[1]

Perhaps some would argue that this is in the nature of the case impossible, and in any event, undesirable. This, they would feel, is to take the heart out of religious education and to reduce it to the level of just another 'subject' in the curriculum when it ought to be touching deeper springs in the children's experience. The answer is that the one does not preclude the other; on the contrary, the one is the necessary preliminary to the other. If it is really to 'touch deeper springs' in children's experience religion must win and keep the intellectual respect of the maturing adolescent as well as touch his feelings. Only if it does both these things will it ultimately also stir the will-to-do. It is true that the teaching of religious knowledge could stop short at the point at which

---

[1] It will be remembered that suggestions were made in chapter 8 as to how such lessons as are here envisaged might be adapted for less able children. The difference is mainly in approach and not so much in the subject-matter.

it remains no more than an intellectual exercise. In practice however, this is not the besetting sin of most religious education; far more often it suffers from a failure to challenge the intellect of the adolescent and seems to him more of an appeal to feelings and action unsupported by convincing intellectual justification. This is an even more important factor when it comes to religious education in VIth Forms, a stage of the work in the secondary school which is considered in some detail in a later chapter.

CHAPTER 10

METHODS OF TEACHING

IT still seems to be necessary, alas, to preface comments on the methods of teaching religious knowledge in school with the reminder that the lessons should normally employ to the full those elements that are basic to all good class-teaching — namely, the active co-operation of the pupils, the use of the black-board, and of note-books.

Every child should have a copy of the Bible. There are still a few secondary schools where this is not so and a few where Scripture note-books are not thought to be necessary. Unfortunately there are also some where the teaching rarely departs from Bible-reading and questions and comment, with little or no use of the black-board or of other teaching methods which would certainly be employed, where appropriate, if the lessons were anything else but 'Scripture'. In addition to rendering the religious knowledge teaching less effective in itself, this marked difference between the method used in the teaching of Scripture and the methods and aids used in the teaching of other subjects in the curriculum, implies in the child's mind that the one is less important than the others. This contributes to the lack of interest in religious education on the part of young people of which mention has already been made. Since religious knowledge is going to be taught in the class-room, let it be taught with all the freshness and variety which can be imparted to any lesson by means of the fullest use of all the methods and teaching aids which are appropriate.

METHODS IN THE JUNIOR SCHOOL

It was suggested in an earlier chapter that the two main

aims of religious teaching in the junior school were to interest the child in carefully selected stories from the Bible and the story of Christianity, and to help him to build up in some detail a picture of the land and people of Palestine in Old and New Testament times. To a large extent these aims help to determine the kind of methods which are appropriate to the teaching at this level.

The teacher will need to cultivate, especially in the first two years, the art of telling Bible and other stories. As the ability to read develops among a particular group of children, so the stories can be increasingly read by the children themselves but the change will be gradual and with some groups will come about more quickly than with others.

There is no need here to go into details of the art of story-telling, which is discussed fully in most books dealing with the work of the teacher in the junior school. There are, however, two points about the telling of religious stories in particular to which attention ought to be drawn. Bible stories are not about men and women who were morally and religiously superior to their fellows, but about ordinary men and women for whom the experience of God was real and important. Stories about them need, therefore, to be told in a matter-of-fact manner and not in a tone of voice, or with an artificial emphasis upon their virtues, which contrive to turn them, in the child's mind, into superior beings who seem far removed from ordinary people. There is, of course, a particular tendency for this to happen in connection with the telling of stories about Jesus. The motive here is doubtless worthy and defensible, but if the aim is to teach the child about Jesus *as man,* as a real person — and this should be the aim at this stage — then the teacher should be content to do just that.

Secondly, Bible stories and stories about great Christians of later days are important, of course, not simply as stories but because they exemplify ideals and virtues and attitudes in action, as it were. It is a nice point for any teacher to decide how best to let the story itself emphasise these things without recourse to a series of verbalised abstractions about 'faith', 'love', 'trust', 'sin', 'repentance' and the like, which can have little or no significance for the child at this stage and which, in any case, quickly cause the children's interest to evaporate. If the story has been well chosen and well told it will itself have conveyed something of its deeper implications. Moreover, the children can be encouraged to talk about the people who figure in it and the things they did and said.

The teacher will be able to judge to what extent it is possible to follow up the story with a reading of it in the Bible itself. Some teachers believe that such reading should be done at first from one of the abridged Bibles and the full Bible used for the first time in the top classes of the junior school. The advantage of this arrangement, they argue, is that selected Bible stories can be read from attractively bound books, printed in large type, and with appropriate headings, instead of in the somewhat dull and forbidding full Bible, with its small print. Others, however, take the view that from the first children should become familiar with the Bible itself, rather than with part of it. This view has certainly gained support now that there is at least one version of the complete Bible which is attractive to look at, has the more widely-read passages printed in larger type than the rest, and is furnished with accurate line-drawings and maps.[1] A Bible which incorporates all these features goes a long way towards making abridged versions superfluous.

Reading from the Bible can often be done dramatically. That is to say, where the passage introduces the reported speech of different characters, it can be read in parts by different children. Three or four voices together can read the words of groups, or 'the people', and a narrator (often the teacher) reads the connecting parts of the passage. This is a

[1] The Authorised Version illustrated by John Stirling, published by the British and Foreign Bible Society in a cheap school edition. For details of abridged Bibles, see Bibliography.

method much enjoyed by younger children who with a little practice can become quite proficient in its use.

Various kinds of follow-up work can be done by the junior child. The miming of action-stories can be done at this age in a class-room with considerable interest and enjoyment on the part of the children who take part and of the others who watch. The parables of the Gospels, in particular, frequently lend themselves to this kind of expression-work. The making of illustrated note-books is another useful piece of work which young children enjoy, in the compilation of which drawing in colour, and painting, probably play a more important part than writing.

All these varied forms of teaching demand of the teacher a fairly full and accurate knowledge of Palestinian geography, life and customs, and of the life and times of people who figure in stories about Christianity in later periods. This too, is the kind of 'social history' upon which the teacher will need to draw heavily for the more deliberate teaching about the land of Palestine, its people and customs, in Old and New Testament times, which it has been suggested should form one of the main tasks in the last two years of the junior school. It should be done in considerable detail, with the aid of authentic pictures, film-strips and films, and with a generous allocation of time for the drawing of pictures, simple maps, and the making of models. It is not, of course, implied that this work be done in isolation from the Bible. On the contrary, it should be developed out of the detail lying behind the stories with which the child will by now have become familiar, and proceed with the addition of further references to other parts of the Bible, so that the background details come to be associated in the child's mind with particular stories and parts of the Bible. By this means, stories from the New Testament, in particular, will become so much more than just 'good stories'. The child will see that they have to do with real people. Because the Centurion, or Jairus, or the Good Samaritan, or Zacchaeus thus become more life-like to him, so will he the more easily perceive that they have something in common with people today.

With the children in the upper part of the junior school, it is sometimes effective to work backwards, as it were, from present-day people and events back to the Bible. Interesting work may be done by taking the life of some recent or contemporary missionary, finding out about his or her life, about the church or country overseas where he has worked, and from that come back to the New Testament story of discipleship and what it means. Likewise the children may be interested in such Societies as the Save the Children Fund, International Help for Children, or the work among children undertaken by the United Nations, and from there go back to what Jesus had to say about children and about those less fortunate than ourselves.

METHODS IN THE SECONDARY SCHOOL

The reading and discussion of selected parts of the Bible are bound to play a central part in the majority of religious knowledge lessons at this level. It follows that every child should possess and be required to make full use of his copy of the Bible, in a rendering which comes as near to contemporary English as possible. It is also advisable that the same version should be used by all the children in a class. The use of different versions in one class can be confusing for the children and is certainly time-wasting for the teacher. Opinions differ as to the best version for this purpose amongst those that are available. Some teachers feel that the advantages of the illustrations in the school edition which is published by the British and Foreign Bible Society outweigh the disadvantage that the text is that of the Authorised Version. Others are willing to forego the illustrations for the sake of the near-contemporary English of the Revised Standard Version.[1]

---

[1] It has to be remembered that the English of the New English Bible, though contemporary in style, is not on that account necessarily easier of comprehension for younger children.

A passage from the Bible can be 'read' in class by four or five different methods. It is not necessary to adhere closely to the method of reading around the class. The teacher may occasionally prefer to read a passage himself on the first occasion, particularly if it is one of those outstanding pieces from the Bible which the children ought to hear read well when they come to it for the first time. Under this head come such passages as David's lament over Saul and Jonathan in 2 Samuel chapter 1, or the call of Isaiah, in Isaiah chapter 6, or the Beatitudes in the Gospels, or St. Paul's hymn to love, in 1 Corinthians 13. On these occasions, indeed, there may well be something to be said in favour of the teacher reading first from the smooth-flowing, melodious English of the Authorised Version.

The method of dramatic reading, already referred to, can still be used successfully in the first two years of the secondary school but is inappropriate with older pupils who have become more self-conscious about such activities. At secondary school level, where the reading of the passage is usually the prelude to the study of facts and ideas underlying it, there is much to be said for following a first dramatic reading by a second, at a later stage in the lesson, when some comment and discussion has taken place on it, and by a different group of children.

In the upper part of the secondary school the method of individual study of Bible passages could well be used much more often than it is. This does not mean that a class of 13-14 year-olds can simply be told to read a certain section and left to get on with it. More often than not the six or seven minutes thus allocated would become a period of increasing fidgeting and noise and be an almost complete waste of time. The passage should be noted on the black-board, concise directions given as to the time to be allowed, and it should be made clear that either written or oral questions about the significant points in the passage will follow. Even more satisfactory will the study become if some of the most important of these points are noted on the black-board, or attention drawn to them orally, before the full reading starts, and the pupils told to discover certain details connected with them from their study of the appropriate verses or sections. By this means point and purpose is given to the individual reading of the passage, which is infinitely to be preferred to a vague and undigested glossing over of the verses. The questions which are then put, either orally or in the form of a short written test, must be pressed home so that the need for thoughtful and attentive study of the text is seen to be important. Vague or superficial answers must be rejected and the pupil made to look again more carefully at the passage until he, and through him, the class generally, get into the habit of tackling this kind of Bible reading with effort and imagination.

It is occasionally useful to get a class to work in groups of six to eight, each studying a part of a section of the Bible with a view to compiling answers to questions set out by the teacher beforehand on a slip of paper, or to constructing a brief scene in a dramatised version of some part of the Bible story. The teacher's planning beforehand of the aims of the work of each group in relation to the total object of the lesson as a whole is here extremely important. Extemporisation on the spur of the moment is particularly to be deplored: it inevitably results in slipshod work and can cause acute embarrassment when the pupils confront the teacher with questions of detail for which he is not prepared. The teacher's contribution during the lesson will be made, of course, by his sitting in with the various groups, guiding and stimulating the study and clearing up any problems or questions which crop up. The particular value of group work of this kind lies not only in the fact that it offers the opportunity of greater activity than usual on the part of the whole class, but also that a group has to commit to writing the information which it is required to gather. The members find that they want all sorts of further details and in this way they are led to fuller understanding of facts and/or insights which in the course of the more conventional type of lesson might easily pass them by.

The value of well-planned written work on the part of the secondary school pupil is recognised by educationists. It encourages more exact formulation of ideas and expression of facts and also offers yet another opportunity of getting the physically active co-operation of the class in learning. It follows that religious knowledge lessons should include a reasonable amount of written work and not be largely confined to oral methods of teaching. Nor need such written work be limited to the more obvious essay-type of homework on the one hand and to the writing up of notes in class on the other, even though these are both valuable in their proper place. A wider range of written work is appropriate to the subject and can help to give greater significance to the teaching as a whole. Where certain facts have had to be learned, a short written test done in rough note-books will serve more effectively to underline the degree of care and attention required than will a few casual oral questions. For 1st and 2nd years greater interest on the part of children can often be stimulated by telling them to imagine that they were present on some occasion about which they have been reading and tell what they saw (or heard, or felt). The writing of a brief playlet about a Biblical event or incident is another form of written work which younger children enjoy.

Older secondary school pupils should be encouraged to keep their own careful notes on important topics and these should be seen regularly by the teacher and discussed with the pupils. Essays to be done by pupils in upper streams should be such as require exact knowledge and serious thought, and ideally, demand reference to books in the school library. Better that three good essays a term of this sort should be done than six or ten at a level which contrasts unfavourably in quality and quantity with those which are expected in connection with other aspects of the curriculum. Diagrams can also usefully be given to supplement certain parts of the teaching, setting out, for instance, the literary relationships between the sources underlying the Synoptic Gospels, or the 'cycle' of sin-oppression-repentance-deliverance which is the theological framework in which the history of the Judges is set. Occasionally also, pupils at this level have produced longer plays of a surprisingly high quality on such themes as a modern re-interpretation of some of the New Testament parables.

The black-board plays an important part in most lessons and, again, the religious knowledge lesson should be no exception. It is just as true of Scripture as it is of other forms of teaching that the sight of words, of sentences summarising an important point, and of an orderly summary of all the main data of a lesson, give a visual reinforcement to the spoken word. So far as the teaching of religion is concerned, this holds good whether the lesson is dealing with more straightforward facts, such as the date of the fall of Samaria or the names which Hosea gave to his children, or is concerned with ideas or themes. Thus, a good, clear black-board summary of the most important parts of the message of Amos, or the meaning of the parable of Dives and Lazarus, or of the conclusions reached by the Christian Council of Jerusalem reported in Acts chapter 15, is both an incentive to clear and concise teaching, and of considerable assistance to the children in clarifying and remembering the ideas or points of view involved. Any teacher who consistently neglects the black-board in the course of divinity teaching needs seriously to ask himself whether this is because his teaching lacks precision and clarity of thought and presentation.

The black-board should also be used to illustrate the places and movements of various sorts which figure prominently in so much Scripture teaching. With a little practice the coast-line of Palestine, and the North-South line of the Jordan with the Lake of Chinnereth (Galilee in New Testament times) and the Dead Sea, can quickly be drawn with sufficient accuracy. If the class is learning about Jesus preaching in the synagogue at Nazareth then Nazareth should be inserted on the map. The attacks of the Philistines in the time of Samuel and Saul can be illustrated by arrows; Paul's route from Jerusalem to Damascus marked in coloured chalk, and so on. Teachers who are skilled in black-board sketching can outline sketches of important archæological data such as the Moabite Stone, the stone figure of Ba'al, the type of jar in which the Dead Sea Scrolls were found.

At certain points in many lessons more accurate and detailed consultation of printed maps will be essential. Indeed, there are very few lessons on the Bible in which some reference to such a map could not usefully be made. The large wall-maps need to be supplemented by individual Bible Atlases, so that children may explore geographical details for themselves to which the teacher draws attention on the large wall-map. Reference to this kind of detail needs to be made more frequently than is sometimes the case: it is all too easy for names of places mentioned in connection with Hebrew or Christian history to become and remain mere verbalisations. Some useful maps and atlases are available.[1]

Pictures can play a most useful part in connection with religious education at the secondary stage. Apart from paintings by great artists, which are mentioned in chapter 11 in relation to VIth Form courses, these will usually be in the nature of photographs or accurate reconstructions of a geographical, archæological, historical or contemporary kind. Photographs of the Wilderness of Judæa, the Lake of Galilee with its surrounding hills, of the walls of ancient Jericho, of the pottery and figures unearthed during recent excavations on the site of Hazor, or in the course of the excavations at Ur, of the entrance to the water-tunnel built under Jerusalem by Hezekiah, of the ruins of a Synagogue at Capernaum, or of a stretch of Roman road along which St. Paul almost certainly travelled; of a statue of Diana, goddess of the Ephesians; of a double-page of the famous Codex Sinaiticus — these and other similar illustrations help to bring vividly to life the background to the Bible and to convey to young

[1] See Bibliography.

people a sense of the solid reality of the people and events of which it speaks. Courses dealing with the later story of Christianity are enlivened by collections of photographs of some of Europe's most famous churches and cathedrals; of people, churches, customs and worship in the Church of South India or of some part of Africa.

The practical difficulty of effectively presenting comparatively small pictures to a class of twenty or more is best overcome by preparing sets of pictures mounted, with short captions, on large sheets of thin board. The sheets can be displayed in a class-room for several days and pupils be encouraged to examine them fully at leisure. At least two inexpensive and reasonably representative books of photographs of archæological finds which bear on the Bible are available and a set of these can be taken from class to class and used as a supporting text-book.[1] The British Museum publishes a number of post-card size photographs of some of the more important of the Biblical archæological exhibits which are housed there and these make up into attractive and useful wall-displays. Photographs of cathedrals and churches are best collected, of course, during holidays and shorter excursions and they too may form the basis of a valuable series of displays.

The film-strip is technically the simplest way of presenting the various types of illustrative material to which reference has been made. A glance at the Bibliography will show just how wide is the range of topics connected with religious education on which film-strips are available. It should be emphasised, however, that they vary both in type and in technical quality and therefore need to be examined and selected with great care. For the purposes of secondary school teaching, those which are most useful are the ones which, like pictures, are made up of authentic material of one kind or another. Those which attempt an imaginative reconstruction of Bible stories, or are dominated by an obvious evangelistic purpose, are hardly appropriate to the

[1] See Bibliography.

kind of work which the secondary school will be attempting to do in the field of religious education. From among those which contain appropriate material the teacher still needs to make a careful selection on the basis of technical quality of the pictures and of the way in which they are presented. It should also be pointed out that for the most effective use of good film-strips, the religious education teacher needs to be familiar with the techniques of film-strip presentation in a class.[1]

Few really good films, unfortunately, have been made which are of a suitable type and length for use in connection with religious education in the secondary school. A selection of those which are available and have been used to good purpose by many teachers will be found listed in the Bibliography. Even more than the film-strip, the film needs to be used, if it is to be an effective aid to good religious education, with a clear understanding of the particular purpose which it can be made to serve and of the follow-up work which a class ought to do when they have seen it for the first time.

All forms of pictures are, inevitably, a substitute for the real thing and when the real thing can itself be seen, it is infinitely to be preferred as a teaching 'aid'. Thus, a visit to a museum, to an ancient parish church or a great cathedral, can create interest and provide the starting-point for a great deal of teaching and learning. Two or three hours spent in a lecture-tour of some of the galleries of the British Museum can do more to bring to life the story of Ur of the Chaldees, the Assyrian and Persian empires which successively dominated and influenced Israel, or the history of the writing and translation of the Bible, than all the hours spent on these topics in the class-room. The history which is reflected in the architecture, furnishings and story of an ancient parish church or of a great Norman cathedral can present a vivid picture of the part which Christianity has played in the various centuries of English life and history

1 On this see Bibliography.

and so tell directly a good deal about the story of Christianity itself.

For such visits the teacher needs, of course, to do a good deal of preparation. For a museum visit, for instance, the teacher needs to pay one or more preliminary visits and to read up the history and significance of the objects to which the children's attention is to be drawn. For a visit, or series of visits, to a church or cathedral a considerable amount of information needs to be acquired, not only about the history of the building itself, but also about the historical happenings which are connected with it. Most of the great cathedrals have had their own historians whose studies of the cathedral and its history deserve to be read with care as part of the preparation for a visit. A memorial tablet, or a tomb, may be the tangible reminder of a whole episode of English history. Thus, the earliest history of Ely Cathedral is connected with the name of St. Etheldreda, about whose life and that of her sister St. Withberga, a great deal of fascinating material has accumulated. But probably the only tangible remains of the very early period in the cathedral's history is to be seen in part of a Saxon-age stone cross bearing an inscription to the memory of St. Etheldreda's steward Ovin. The labour involved in preparing adequately for such expeditions can, of course, be lightened if it can be shared with an historian on the school staff. That this preparatory work and planning is well worth the effort and time which they demand has been proved in the experience of teachers who have attempted such visits and seen for themselves the interest and enthusiasm which they have evoked in the children.

The value, as well as the difficulties, of discussion-lessons conducted with classes of adolescents have been considered at some length in an earlier chapter.[1] It is only necessary here to stress the fact that this method of teaching could usefully be employed in the upper part of the secondary school as generously as circumstances will allow.

Effective religious education at the secondary school stage

[1] See chapter 7.

demands, above all, the provision of an adequate supply of the right kind of books about religion in the school library. There are expensive but important books of reference to which children should be able to be referred for further information, or for study which they are required to do on particular aspects of the work. For VIth Forms, as will be noted below, this kind of provision is essential but it is often highly desirable for effective work from the 4th form upwards. Ideally, a secondary school library should contain a set of Hastings' Dictionary of the Bible — a mine of accurate information about all the important items mentioned in the Bible — and perhaps also a set of the Encyclopædia of Religion and Ethics, which deals with religion from a standpoint very much wider than that of Christianity alone. One of the larger Bible Atlases, and two or three of the larger Bible Commentaries are also essential. These need to be supplemented by the inclusion of standard works on the separate books of the Bible, on the history of Israel, the theology of the Old Testament and the New, the history of the Church in earlier and later times, the Churches today, the story of the Bible, and Biblical archæology. It is also necessary to include a number of books which attempt to explain the meaning of Christianity in terms of modern thought, and books dealing with, and containing translations of some parts of the sacred writings of, the other great living religions of the world. So much fresh literature on all these topics appears each year that teachers need help in keeping abreast of it and in deciding what, from among all that appears, could usefully be added to the library. They will find a good deal of initial help in a *Bibliography for Teachers of Religious Knowledge* published by the Institute of Christian Education, and in the various journals which contain notices of recent publications in these various fields.[1]

This chapter has been concerned with the various kinds of teaching techniques which the teacher of religious knowledge can employ. Obviously the best techniques in the world in

[1] See Bibliography.

the hands of a poor teacher will not guarantee that he teaches well. Ideally, he must be a good teacher using as many good techniques as possible (though even a poor teacher will produce a somewhat better lesson if he is trying to use the best techniques). Methods of teaching are but tools in the hands of the teacher. In words which have since become famous, Sir Winston Churchill once pleaded: 'Give us the tools and we will finish the job'. The good teacher of religious knowledge cannot afford to ignore the tools he is using. He will certainly do a good job even better if he makes the fullest and widest use of the various methods which have been touched upon in this chapter.

APPENDIX

RELIGIOUS SOCIETIES IN SCHOOLS

IN the last fifteen years or so it has become increasingly common for secondary schools to have among their voluntary groups meeting after school hours a religious society of one sort or another. In some schools the society is a group with no affiliations outside the school; but probably the majority nowadays are parts of one of the larger movements — the Schools' Christian Union or the S.C.M. in Schools Movement. In the case of these last, the school society operates, as do the others, as a voluntary group within the school, but also combines from time to time with groups from other schools in central activities organised by the two movements. Thus, area meetings of the S.C.M. in Schools are held from time to time which are attended by groups from affiliated schools in that area. By this means young people can listen to talks from distinguished speakers who would not be available to each school society and can also enjoy inter-change of ideas and the sense of fellowship which are possible at these larger gatherings.

Religious societies in schools have come into existence because they provide young people with the chance of meeting with members of the school staff and with people from outside the school and exchanging ideas in a more informal manner than is possible in the course of ordinary Divinity lessons. Because membership is voluntary, it follows that the youngsters who join do so because religion is a matter of interest or concern to them. The fact that this interest can be taken for granted at the meetings of the group tends to make for a somewhat freer and more positive atmosphere than is often the case during classroom discussion of religious matters. From the point of view of those members of the staff who choose to attend meetings of the society, opportunities are provided of discovering more about the ideas, problems and difficulties of some of the adolescents who come, and of thus doing more to guide and assist than they might otherwise be able to do. The fact that other members of the staff than those whose official task it is to teach Divinity choose to come and join in discussions, adds considerably to the influence which the group can exert on its adolescent members. It is made clear to them that religion matters to people who spend their time teaching 'secular' subjects as well as to those who teach religion.

The main purpose of such a society is to help to foster the religious development of young people in various ways. In some groups a good deal of attention is given to the devotional reading of the Bible and to prayer. Films are shown and discussed. In all, the attempt is made to consider and discuss the meaning and implications of the Christian faith for the lives of the youngsters who are its members. Visiting speakers sometimes include the local clergy and ministers and in this way a valuable link is made between the school and the local churches.

A very important feature of most groups is the undertaking by the members of some form of social service as an expression of Christian charity. The emphasis here is on the giving of time and effort — working a shopping rota for local old people in the lunch-hour, helping in a local children's home, visiting elderly or bed-ridden people, and so on. Frequently youngsters are attracted to the group in the first place through this emphasis on serving the community and in certain cases less-gifted members of a group come to feel that by such means they can make a real contribution to its activities.

In 1955 the Student Christian Movement in Schools, which had until then found its main centre of work in the grammar schools, began an experiment to discover what sort of a response could be found in secondary modern schools. With the support of the Lancashire, Liverpool and Manchester Education Authorities it organised groups in the modern schools in those areas. It was soon clear that many of these schools and the pupils in them welcomed the formation of their own religious societies. Since then, the movement has grown and now embraces a considerable number of schools in various parts of the country.[1]

[1] An account of the beginnings of the work and some reflections on its results four years later by The Revd. Eric Lord, who initiated it, can be read in *Religion in Education*, Vol. 26, No. 3, Summer, 1959.

CHAPTER 11

SIXTH FORM PROBLEMS

No apology is needed for the manner in which the chapter-heading here chosen puts the emphasis on the *problems* connected with religious education in sixth forms. Those teachers who have to interest large mixed sixth forms, made up often of Arts and Science 'A' level pupils, in religion in one short period a week, know only too well just how formidable the task is and how many acute problems it throws up for them, in the planning as well as the conduct of the lessons.

The problems are commonly four in number. First there is the lack of concern among many of the pupils for a subject which can be given but one period a week, and has to be taken in groups far too large, because no more time can be spared from among the 'A' level courses which are the primary concern of both staff and pupils at this stage. This means that, with a few exceptions, the general attitude of sixth form pupils to religious education is to regard it as a nuisance — an unnecessary interruption of more important work. Nor does it help the teacher responsible for religious education at this level to remind himself that a similar view is usually taken of other 'fringe' subjects, like art and music.

Moreover secondly, the sixth form teacher dealing with religion is aware that he is presenting it, in any normal group, to a fairly large number of young people who are already beginning to find themselves out of sympathy with the religious point of view. There is some evidence to suggest that at about age 17 most adolescents reach a crisis in the process of shaping their attitudes to religious beliefs and practices and that this crisis is resolved, one way or the other, by about the age of 20.[1] Present indications are that a minority, and not the majority, of young people come to and through this sort of crisis favourably disposed towards the more conventional type of religious beliefs and practices. Obviously therefore, teachers are going to be made aware of dissenting attitudes and beliefs in the lower as well as the upper sixth forms.

In the third place, there are problems for the teacher in the matter of deciding what aims are appropriate to his work in these two years. On the one hand the Agreed Syllabuses assume that the teaching at this level should rest on the basis of that done in previous years and aim at a broadening as well as a deepening of the earlier teaching. For the minority of the pupils whose attitudes to Christianity are favourable this is clearly the right sort of aim to have in mind. At the same time, it plainly will not get the teacher very far with the majority who are growing further away from the Christian point of view in their thinking and attitudes. For this group the teacher may well feel that he has to attempt something like a final presentation of the claims of religion and the religious attitude to life, since this may well be the last occasion on which some of these young people will be likely to be confronted with a reasoned and systematic challenge of this sort. The need for this dual aim in sixth form religious education presents the teacher with one of his most knotty problems.

Finally, there is the problem whether to put the main emphasis on the intellectual foundations and defence of religion or on the more practical bearing of religion on life. Young people, the teacher may well feel, want to see that religion really works — that it is not just something for those of a pious disposition, or who are in the habit of going to church on Sundays. On the other hand, he is aware that his teaching is being given to young people who are mostly pre-occupied with intellectual pursuits of one kind or another,

[1] See M. Argyle, *Religious Behaviour*, London, 1958, esp. pp. 58–70.

many of whom are going to become thoughtful people whose religion must carry intellectual conviction, as well as touch emotions and will, if it is to continue to be a force in their lives. Few of them are likely to engage in systematic study of religion after they leave school. This may well be the last chance of deepening somewhat the intellectual foundations of their religious ideas and attitudes.

It is little wonder, then, that those who are responsible for the religious education in sixth forms soon become aware of the problems which it throws up for them. The Crowther Report seems to have had such problems very much in mind, as well as the importance of getting to grips with them, when it stressed the part which religious education of the right kind could and should play in the work of sixth forms.

> 'Needs that all sixth formers have in common . . . (include) religious instruction — or, rather, the very much wider field of everything that contributes to the formation of moral standards. . . . All sixth formers also share a common spiritual heritage. They bring to it many different attitudes. The approach, and the recoil, of the history specialist and the science specialist are likely to be different but complementary. . . . There is much to be gained from making the periods set apart for this purpose periods in which arts and science specialists can join together — provided that the members of the group know each other well enough to make discussion profitable . . . the reason they come together is common to both. It is the endeavour to discover and to understand the central affirmations of the Christian faith so that (whether they accept it or not) they at least may know what Christians believe.'[1]

Up to about fifteen or twenty years ago it used to be fairly commonly assumed that it was the task primarily of the headmaster or headmistress to take the sixth forms for Divinity. No doubt there are some heads who still do so but it is becoming increasingly common for this task to be

---

[1] *Fifteen to Eighteen*, Report of the Central Advisory Council for Education, England, H.M.S.O. 1959, paras. 408–9.

entrusted to the Divinity specialist. The reason for this change is, of course, that few heads of schools have the qualifications, or have had the time to do the necessary reading, to allow them to teach religion at the kind of level which they realise sixth form pupils need and to which they are entitled. This is by no means to suggest that he (or she) cannot make a useful contribution to the work: the very fact that he is prepared and interested enough to join in some of the discussion about religion can help to underline the significance of the course in a way which is most valuable. Since, however, as has already been stressed, these are young people who are being encouraged to develop their intellectual capacities to the full, it follows that the most normal and natural approach to their study of religion will be through the intellectual foundations and aspects of it towards its spiritual importance, and obviously the Divinity specialist should normally be the best person to undertake this kind of work.

The value of the contribution which can be made at this sort of level by a specialist is potentially considerable. Students in Training Colleges and University Departments of Education who have elected to make Divinity one of their courses of study frequently testify to the fact that their interest in religion and their desire to study it to a deeper level arose out of the stimulating quality of the teaching which they received from a teacher in the sixth form who was well-informed and won their respect for the subject.

It would be easy, as well as irritating to the reader, to indulge in clichés about the qualities which a specialist ought to have for this particular task. Two are so important, however, that they cannot escape mention — broad experience and wide sympathies, on the one hand, and high intellectual standards and integrity on the other. The importance of this last quality in the teacher of religion for his work at all levels has been constantly stressed in previous pages. In his work with sixth forms it assumes greater importance because of the emphasis which, it has been suggested, needs to be put upon the intellectual foundations and justification of religion in this part of the school course. While it is true that people seldom seem to argue their way intellectually, as it were, into belief in God, the fact remains that many young people in middle and later adolescence find religion unattractive because they feel that it cannot stand up to rigorous intellectual scrutiny. If a Divinity teacher can at least succeed in winning the respect of sixth formers for his own academic standards and scholarship, they are more likely to be ready to concede that religion is, after all, worthy of serious consideration.

Perhaps the main occupational hazard of the specialist Divinity teacher, however, is that of becoming theologically conditioned, in modes of thought and in manner of expression. This is calculated to cut him off from the pupils who are unsympathetic to religion more quickly and decisively than anything else. However convinced he may be himself of the rightness of the beliefs and practices which are associated with the Christian religion, he must constantly make the effort to see things from the point of view of the pupils to whom religion seems intellectually, emotionally and morally feeble and unconvincing. He will manage to do this only if he takes the trouble to read books, to see films and plays, to listen to broadcasts which, and to meet people who, are critical of, or hostile to religion, as well as those favourably disposed towards it. His is very much a 'frontier' task, so far as sixth forms are concerned, and he must not expect it to be anything else, since he is teaching Divinity in a situation which fully reflects the 'age of perplexity' in which we live.

What course of work, then, should the specialist plan for his sixth forms which will provide real intellectual stimulus for both the incipient believer and unbeliever, and also do something to show the bearing of religion on real life? A glance at four or five of the most widely used of the Agreed Syllabuses will indicate that they do not all, by any means, offer as much help here as one might hope for. Most of them suggest that pupils might study at greater depth than they have yet had the chance to do, some part of the literature of the Old or New Testament, or its theology. Most are also agreed that it would be a good thing to offer a course dealing with the bearing of religion upon personal and social problems. Another and almost universal suggestion, is a course on the other great religions of the world. Some also favour courses on some aspect of the history of the Church in more recent times, and on the Fourth Gospel. Most seem to be agreed that it would be advisable to provide a number of shorter courses on different subjects, rather than longer courses on one or two.

With this last point most sixth form Divinity teachers would probably agree. Three short courses in a year, dealing with different topics each term, offer a better chance of maintaining interest and spreading it more widely over the group. Most teachers would also want to include among such short courses one on Christian belief, another on Religion and Personal and Social Problems, and a third on Other Religions. The first, if presented apologetically and not dogmatically, offers the opportunity of considering the intellectual foundations and justification of the Christian religion and the chance to remove a number of widely accepted but erroneous ideas about what Christianity teaches. The second gives pupils the chance of examining, not only the bearing of Christianity upon daily life, but also their own attitudes to some of the more obvious moral issues which are likely to confront them in the future. The third is a topic of perennial interest on the part of thoughtful young people in these days when Europe is in closer touch with the Middle and the Far East.

There is some evidence to suggest that all three, in fact, are topics upon which many sixth formers would themselves most prefer to have guidance and discussion. A recent report of *An Enquiry into the Methods and Effects of Religious Education in Sixth Forms,* published by the University of Nottingham Institute of Education, reveals that Social

Problems, Doctrinal matters, Comparative Religion[1], and Religion and Philosophy, in this order, were subjects which Training College students would most have liked to discuss as part of their Divinity courses in the sixth form at school.[2]

Another topic which is of interest to sixth formers is that of the distinctive beliefs and practices connected with some of the 'Deviations' from the main Christian tradition — Christian Science, British Israelites, the Church of the Latter Day Saints (the Mormons), the Seventh Day Adventists and Jehovah's Witnesses.

Many schools make use of the B.B.C. broadcasts for sixth forms called *The Christian Religion and Its Philosophy.* Each year a number of eminent thinkers and scholars contribute talks on certain themes which can form the basis for useful discussion. It will be evident that in order to make the fullest use of such talks and ensure that later discussion is profitable, the teacher himself has to do a certain amount of special reading. The talks themselves are therefore in the nature of expert aids to, and not substitutes for, the teacher's own contribution.

There are certainly some schools in which the sixth form courses include a study of the Fourth Gospel. Its value, especially where it involves the reading of one or two good books and the writing of the occasional essay, is potentially very great. On the other hand, for reasons already suggested, other teachers would feel that it would be extremely difficult, if not impossible, to get very far with this kind of course. In view of this, it is particularly important to remember that courses in which the attempt is made to examine the influence of religion upon certain aspects of music, painting,

---

[1] This is also a topic on which many Divinity teachers particularly feel the need for guidance in the matter of reading and the planning of the course. They will find some detailed suggestions in the author's booklet *Teaching Children about World Religions,* Harrap, 1961.

[2] 1962, p. 31. Teachers responsible for sixth form Divinity will find a good deal of interesting information in this Report about the attitudes of young people to the religious education which was provided in their sixth forms and its impact upon them.

architecture and literature can be both interesting and extremely valuable for sixth forms Obviously such courses start with the initial advantage that they represent a fresh approach compared with the Biblical — or Church History — based approach which has of necessity dominated the teaching in earlier years. They have a special appeal to those among the pupils who happen to be interested in one or other of these subjects. They open up the possibility that the co-operation of other members of the staff can be enlisted, thus giving to the course greater variety and, still more important, expert guidance and comment in the particular field.

Many teachers would feel that a list of suggested short courses would be incomplete without mention of one on Science and Religion. It is obviously important that at a time when the conflict between the two is less talked of because Science is so much in the ascendant, but none the less real for all that, some time should be given to showing what the relation is between the scientific and the religious view of the world. Done properly, this is a demanding piece of work and should be conducted with the co-operation of one or more of the scientists on the school staff. There are, however, some Divinity teachers who would feel that such a course as this can often fall rather flat because at this stage the wider implications of Science, as distinct from the details which sixth formers are studying in Physics, Chemistry, or Biology courses, are as yet hardly perceived. Even so, much can be done to enable pupils to become a little more 'literate' or 'numerate' (to adapt the terminology so aptly used by the Crowther Report), as the case may be, at the points where Science and Religion seem to impinge upon each other.

Finally, a word ought to be said about methods of teaching in connection with sixth form Divinity courses. There is a temptation for the teacher who wants to get as much as possible into the one period a week allowed, to do most of the teaching himself, with a proportion of the time in most lessons allotted to discussion. In certain cases, this is advisable and sometimes almost inevitable, because his reading and knowledge of the subject under discussion are required to lay the foundation which any useful discussion requires. It must be remembered, however, that the more the pupils can themselves be encouraged to read and prepare notes for a lesson, the more can this part of the teaching conform to the kind of pattern which sixth form work aims to set. It is infinitely more valuable that the pupils should discover for themselves, through an hour or two spent in the library on recommended books, what are the facts with which they have to come to terms in order to understand what is involved in some part of religious belief, or practice, or history and the like, than that they should get it from the teacher in the form of a 'lecturette'. The business of beginning to discover at first-hand what books have been written on religious topics and the kind of facts and/or points of view which are set forth in them, is as important a part of the proper activities of the sixth-former taking Divinity (even as an 'extra') as it is of his work in other academic subjects which are his main concern. It follows, of course, that it is the responsibility of the Divinity teacher to ensure that the school library includes the kind of volumes which make this possible.

CHAPTER 12

G.C.E. EXAMINATIONS IN RELIGIOUS KNOWLEDGE

THE number of candidates entering for the G.C.E. examinations who have included Religious Knowledge among their subjects has shown a steady, even if not a striking, increase in recent years, both at 'O' and at 'A' Level. The following table makes this clear and also sets out the comparable totals for Geography and History candidates — two subjects which come nearer to Religious Knowledge than most of the others in the secondary school curriculum in respect of allocation of time and relative degree of importance.

'O' LEVEL

Year	Religious Knowledge					
	Entered		Passed		Entered	Passed
	Boys	Girls	Boys	Girls	Totals	
1956	9,507	19,563	4,499	12,342	29,070	16,841
1961	16,003	30,533	6,898	19,378	46,536	26,276

Year	Geography		History	
	Entered	Passed	Entered	Passed
1956	88,708	50,215	86,547	51,297
1961	125,949	68,399	120,413	70,265

'A' LEVEL

Year	Religious Knowledge					
	Entered		Passed		Entered	Passed
	Boys	Girls	Boys	Girls	Totals	
1956	342	851	228	669	1,193	897
1961	689	1,776	407	1,298	2,465	1,705

Year	Geography		History	
	Entered	Passed	Entered	Passed
1956	8,509	6,256	11,997	9,015
1961	13,255	9,263	17,831	13,159[1]

Three facts which emerge from an examination of these figures call for special mention. (1) Though it is true that there has been a steady increase in the number of candidates taking G.C.E. examinations in most subjects at both levels, the rate of growth in Religious Knowledge has increased to a greater extent than is the case with some other subject-entries. This would seem to imply that more schools now think it worth while to make provision for specialist teaching of Divinity at fifth and sixth form levels and to encourage pupils to offer it in the examinations. (2) Between two and three times as many girls as boys offer Religious Knowledge in these examinations and the proportion of the boys who pass is noticeably smaller than that of the girls at 'O' Level, and rather smaller at 'A' Level. The implication here is either that the boys find the examinations more difficult than the girls (which is hard to accept) or that there are rather more weaker candidates from boys' schools offering the subject than from girls' schools. (3) The proportion of all candidates who obtain a pass in the examinations, at 'O' and 'A' Level,

[1] Figures taken from Ministry of Education Statistics for these two year. H.M.S.O.

is about the same as in most other subjects. This fact would seem to be an adequate comment on the suggestion, still occasionally heard, that it is 'easier' for a candidate to obtain a pass in this subject than in some other subjects.

The fact that comparatively few pupils offer Religious Knowledge in these examinations as compared with most other subjects, is accounted for to some extent by the fact that teachers are not all agreed that religious education can or should be made the subject of formal examination. Those who argue against such examinations usually do so on one of two grounds. It is said that no examination can in fact test young people's grasp and appreciation of something so essentially personal as religion and that the very title of such examinations as are held, 'Religious *Knowledge*', itself underlines this fact. It is also argued that to make religious education in school into a course ending in a formal examination comparable in young people's minds with other 'subjects' in the curriculum, is to encourage a wholly erroneous idea as to the nature and purpose of religious education. It is, indeed, to turn it into an academic study, when it ought to be going very much deeper and be the means of encouraging them to come to terms with beliefs, values and attitudes which should profoundly influence their whole development.

With both these objections any teacher who is concerned to make religious education in school as effective as possible is bound to have sympathy. Yet it should be noticed that these objections need more careful scrutiny. Teachers who believe that examinations in Religious Knowledge are, on the whole, a good thing are among the first to agree that they cannot be, nor are meant to be, examinations of young people's total grasp and appreciation of the place and significance of religion, but only of their grasp and understanding of certain facts which should form the foundation of a full appreciation of religion. They point out that so far as the Christian religion is concerned, it has a long history and is rooted in the Bible: it is not the outcome of a purely individual and spontaneous religious tendency without historical and Biblical roots. This being so, there are certain facts, both about the Bible and about the history of Christian belief and practice, which the intelligent young person today ought to be aware of. It is towards the grasp and understanding of these facts that formal examinations in Religious Knowledge can help to provide a useful incentive.

They would many of them go further and argue that, since young people are going to become increasingly occupied, from the 4th secondary year onwards, with G.C.E. examinations and the work that has to be done for them, teaching about religion in school in these later years can run up against increasing difficulties where it is not an examinable subject for G.C.E. It can lack prestige in the children's minds and also actually suffer by a reduction in the amount of time formerly devoted to it in the time-table. This, they maintain, only makes religious education an even more up-hill task than it would ordinarily be in the upper part of the secondary school.

To these contentions, others would add a third, namely that for those who may later want to take Religious Knowledge as a subject in a Training College or University course, the work done for a G.C.E. examination at 'A' Level can be a very valuable preparation. Here they would certainly have the majority of Training College Lecturers in Divinity on their side, who know from experience that their students who have studied Divinity at school to this kind of level are normally able to make much better headway in their Training College Divinity course.

These last are powerful arguments and to them it is necessary to add only one further point. It should not be assumed that because a teacher is helping a group of young people to prepare for a G.C.E. examination in Religious Knowledge, the pupils gain from this part of their work nothing more than a collection of bare, academic facts which have no connection with the deepening of their insight into religion in its spiritual and moral aspects. The two can, and in the hands of the best teachers do, go closely together, especially during the middle and later years of adolescence and for thoughtful youngsters who need, as was pointed out in the last chapter, a deepening of their understanding of the intellectual foundations of religious faith. Of course it is *possible* for a teacher to teach for, and a pupil to prepare for, an examination in Religious Knowledge with no other aim than simply to amass the necessary facts with which to impress the examiners, or because another G.C.E. 'pass' is necessary and this seems the best way in which to get it. The same *possibility* holds for any other subject, including Music or Art. In practice, however, it is difficult to imagine any conscientious teacher tolerating this state of affairs, and the dangers of its happening cannot be allowed to outweigh the immensely valuable gains to be had from the conscientious and scholarly teaching which G.C.E. examinations in Religious Knowledge have done so much to encourage.

The general aims which lie behind the syllabuses, and the examination papers based on them at 'O' and 'A' Level respectively are not vastly different in the case of Religious Knowledge from those in other nearly comparable subjects. A glance at the syllabuses of the various examining bodies and at the papers which are set year by year will show that at 'O' Level it is hoped that the candidate will have gained a reasonably accurate mastery of certain facts connected with the more important parts of the Old and New Testaments and, if the teacher so wishes, about the early history of the Christian Church. He is encouraged, that is, to get to know something of the Bible at first hand and in some detail, and to be able to explain some of the teaching it contains. If he studies the early history of the Church, it is hoped that he will gain from his course some knowledge of the way in which the Christian religion continued to develop in the formative period immediately following the time of the Apostles.

For examinations at 'A' Level, the syllabuses encourage candidates to get to know some of the more obvious matters which have been the subject of scholarly debate and enlightenment, mainly in connection with the Old and New Testaments, and to be able to show how their understanding of the Bible has deepened as a result of this further knowledge about it. Needless to say, this does not imply that candidates are required to be familiar with all the latest pronouncements of contemporary scholars. This is more properly the kind of work which is appropriate to more advanced studies in Training Colleges and Universities. They are, however, expected and encouraged to become familiar with those major developments in the fields of literary criticism, historical studies and archæology in recent years which have been regarded by the majority of scholars as having an important bearing on our knowledge of and understanding of the Bible.

It is worth noticing that in recent years at least two of the examining Bodies, namely Oxford and London, provided in their Scholarship Level syllabuses and examination papers, incentives to a broader and more contemporary type of study. Candidates were expected to read a dozen or so books of a recent kind dealing with two of the following fields of study:

> Science and Religion, World Religions, The Later History of the Christian Church, the Church in England, Biblical Theology, Christian Belief and Conduct.

Unfortunately, the abandonment of the Scholarship Papers has, in one case at any rate, brought to an end this highly desirable attempt to promote the study of wider aspects of religion at this level, with its reference to some of the more important contemporary religious literature. This is to be regretted chiefly because it is essential that young people who are making a serious study of religion at this stage should be encouraged to read outside the limits of Biblical Studies, even though the study of the Bible will doubtless continue, and rightly so, to form the core of their work. There is much to be said for a revision of the 'A' Level syllabuses in Religious

Knowledge which would serve to combine with the Biblical Studies this wider type of reading. If, for instance, two three-hour Papers are to be set for the 'A' Level examination, it would be reasonable to set one combined Paper on Old and New Testament syllabuses, and the second on two or three of these wider aspects of the study of religion — preferably in such a manner that candidates were encouraged in this second paper to write longer essays rather than to 'answer' five or so questions.

It is much to be hoped that schools will do more to make it possible for suitable candidates to take the G.C.E. examinations in Religious Knowledge, particularly at 'A' Level. A pass at 'A' Level counts, of course, for the purposes of scholarships and qualifications for entry to Universities and Training and other Colleges equally with other 'A' Level passes. It has already been made clear that there is much to be said in favour of those who hope to teach undertaking the kind of work which is required for this particular examination. It has considerable value, however, in itself and quite apart from its practical value to a potential teacher, as a general cultural course. The Bible and the Christian religion have exerted so considerable an influence upon the history and the affairs of the English speaking peoples that a serious study of both taken to the sort of standard required in the 'A' Level examination can do much to educate young people in the broadest sense. So far as the school course goes, it combines most satisfactorily with those in English Literature, History and Classics. Perhaps, however, schools should be concerning themselves nowadays less with the more obvious combinations of 'A' Level subjects, than with encouraging their pupils to learn to come to terms with at least one course which differs in content and categories of thought from those which constitute their primary concern.[1]

[1] It will be recalled that it was with something like this aim in mind that the Director of the University of Oxford Institute of Education recently advocated an arrangement by which 'half' subjects could be taken in the 'A' Level examinations.

It is true, of course, that at present there are very real practical difficulties to be faced before a school could feel free to encourage some of its potential scientists to spend time upon a serious study of Divinity which led to an 'A' Level examination in the subject. At the same time it is the case that there are many undergraduates reading Science at the Universities who are profoundly interested in religion and who would have derived considerable assistance in thinking out their religious beliefs, and harmonising them with the rest of their thought and attitudes, if they had undertaken the kind of study which an 'A' Level course in Divinity calls for. It may be argued that the Universities ought to make it possible for the undergraduates who so desire to do this while they are pursuing their undergraduate studies, and there is a good deal to be said for this view. On the whole the University Departments of Theology do far less than their counterparts in the U.S.A. to provide courses designed to improve the general culture of students. But the kind of specialisation which largely accounts for this situation in English Universities does not begin in the Universities so much as in the schools where sixth form work in particular concentrates upon a narrow field of study for the various groups of pupils. No doubt there is a vicious circle here, the Universities exerting pressure upon the schools through entry-standards and the schools making it possible for the Universities to do so by encouraging pupils to work to higher levels along narrower lines. In this situation, not only Divinity studies, but most of the Humanities, tend at present to suffer.

But of the Humanities, it may be asked, why does Divinity tend to be one of the subjects most-neglected in schools at this level? Probably the reason is that on the one hand the 'climate of opinion' nowadays is not favourably disposed towards religion, at an rate in the conventional sense, and on the other, that comparatively few people realise just how far the study of Divinity in its various fields has changed and hardened in the last fifty years or so. It is still largely thought of in terms of the abstruse, highly speculative, system of theological ideas which for centuries it tended to be — and was, in the main, up to the latter part of the last century. During the last fifty years it has undergone a steady transformation of which far too little is known by those who have not had to make a serious study of some part of it. Perhaps it would be given more serious consideration as a valuable part of the education of sixth form pupils if the schools realised that the academic standards associated with it nowadays are every bit as thorough and exacting as are those of any of the Humanities.

It follows from this last point, that in those schools where sixth form courses for G.C.E. 'A' Level examinations in Religious Knowledge are provided, it is usually realised that adequate allocation of time in the time-table has to be made if the course is to achieve its object, not merely in the shape of an examination 'pass', but also in terms of the laying of a good foundation of knowledge and the fostering of the right attitudes and insights. In certain respects indeed, the work at this level can be more exacting in Divinity than in some other subjects. This is principally because pupils have to begin to look at the Bible from a profounder point of view than is immediately apparent to them. What in the Old Testament, looks like history, may be nothing of the sort. As was pointed out in an earlier chapter, a book ascribed to, and given a superficial appearance of belonging to the age of, a particular individual, may be composed of a number of sections which belonged to different periods. Gospels which look like straightforward records of the life and ministry of Jesus may be in part interpretations of a period later than the events of which they speak, with all the important implications which such a fact has for their meaning. Passages which in the Authorised Version of the Bible have been accepted and understood in that form may have been based upon an original text which is now thought to be less reliable than was once assumed.

If an 'A' Level course is doing its job properly, these are

the sort of facts with which it must encourage pupils to begin to get to grips and the implications of which it must help them to begin to see. In some cases, such a course also includes the beginning of the study of part of the New Testament in the original Greek and this can open up for the student something like a different dimension in his appreciation of the meaning of the Gospels and the Epistles. He has also to begin to read for himself some of the best of the general works of scholars and to learn to summarise and work out the implications of the most important of their conclusions in essays.

It will be apparent, therefore, that courses at this level, and with this kind of goal, demand just as much time as can be found for them out of the total allocation for all the 'A' Level courses which a student is pursuing. The work will be both time-consuming and exacting but out of it can come a new appreciation of the Bible and the Christian religion which is rooted in it, and new insights into religion itself, which are to be had in no other way.

G.C.E. examinations are, of course, only some — even if the most important — of the examinations in religious knowledge which are attempted by pupils in secondary schools. Many schools nowadays set regular terminal or yearly tests in the subject as part of their normal internal examinations. The reasons for doing so are those which we have noted already in connection with G.C.E. examinations, and, of course, there are the same objections.

One important point about the internal examinations in religious knowledge however, needs consideration. While there is a strong case for arguing that examinations set by an external examining body are best confined to the testing of largely factual knowledge, on the grounds that they are taken by candidates who are representative of all the major religious denominations, the case is not by any means so strong for confining the school's own examinations within these limits. It has ben shown in an earlier chapter that the teaching and the worship of the School Assembly are together intended to open up to young people the significance and the potentialities for human life of religious faith and experience. It would seem highly desirable therefore, that examinations inside the school should be an incentive to the discussion of the meaning of religion at a deeper level, and not simply tests of factual knowledge. It is certainly important that a 4th year pupil should be able to answer questions which demand a knowledge, and reasonable explanation of the meaning of, say, the main points in the message of Amos or of a parable of Jesus. It is perhaps more valuable, both to the pupil and to the teacher, and certainly more stimulating, that some questions should be set which encourage young people to say whether they can see any meaning in these and other aspects of religious teaching which they have been studying — for people today, and themselves in particular.

It might be objected that this is to encroach upon the freedom of individuals to hold their own religious opinions. The contrary is in fact the case, for it is the ability to make full use of this freedom to ponder the meaning of religion, to think about it critically, or with approval, that the good teacher is trying to encourage. Therefore if the examinations are to be a reflection of the teaching and the work done in the year, it is difficult to see how they can fail to reflect this important aim.

It goes almost without saying that such an aim in the teaching and in an examination, could be achieved only where it was accepted as a basic principle that everyone was quite free to say what he liked, so long as he were making a serious attempt to express a real point of view. This atmosphere of hard reality is precisely what the best teachers of religion want to create, for its existence is evidence that religion is being seriously examined by the young people they are teaching.

CHAPTER 13

CLASSROOM and ASSEMBLY

From the standpoint of adequate provision of religious education, the importance which the Education Act attaches not only to teaching about religion but also to the holding of a daily religious service or Assembly is absolutely correct. Religious education is more than teaching about religion in the classroom: it is also the provision of the opportunity for the child to enter into that fuller religious experience which is to be found in worship. Religion in the full sense touches, as we have said, feelings and will, as well as thought.

In the religious education which goes on in the classroom the emphasis is upon thought — upon ideas of God and the religious man's interpretation of life. In the course of this teaching feelings may sometimes be touched as well — certainly they will be if the teaching is good. It would be hard, for instance, not to be moved by the sufferings which the prophet Jeremiah had to contend with in the course of his work in Judah and Jerusalem. The story of Boaz' kindness to Ruth is also moving and so certainly are some of the parts of the story of St. Paul and of the experiences of Jesus himself. Older pupils may also be moved by some of the finer passages of the Bible, such as David's lament over Saul and Jonathan, or the account of the call of the prophet Isaiah, or St. Paul's Hymn in praise of Christian Love in his first letter to the Corinthians. At the same time, most teachers would feel instinctively that deliberately to attempt to arouse emotion on the part of the children in the course of their classroom teaching about religion is undesirable: if feelings are touched, it will be an incidental and not a calculated result of the lesson.

On the whole, the work in the classroom does not normally provide opportunities for the children to give active expression to their religious ideas and beliefs, except in so far as this can be partially achieved verbally, or in the making of models or the drawing or painting of pictures. In the worship which the school provides through its daily service, however, children can give active expression to their religious beliefs in a manner which allows emotions to come into play as well. Prayers are *said,* in a manner which actively implies recognition of the fact of Almighty God and of man's dependence upon him. Hymns are *sung,* in the course of which active expression can be given to the child's ideas and feelings about God and the world, and himself in relation to both. The use of good music, both in the singing and as a prologue to the service, together with the provision of a suitable setting for it, can go a long way towards creating for the child an 'atmosphere' in which he may become aware of a sense of worship in which some of the deeper emotions are aroused. Thus, classroom and Assembly are, or can be, complementary, so far as religious education is concerned.

It is perhaps necessary to add that the distinction which has here been made between the emphases which are characteristic of religious teaching in the classroom, on the one hand, and of the school service, on the other, are not, of course, absolute. Teaching is also imparted in the Assembly, through hymns, prayers, and the manner in which the service is conducted, just as surely as it is given in the classroom. It is for this reason especially, that the details of the daily act of worship, the choice of hymns and the tunes to which they are sung, the prayers, and the detailed arrangements of the service as a whole, need to be planned with care and imagination. Fortunately, most hymn books which are in use in the schools nowadays omit some of the more obviously unsuitable hymns. It could not have been good, indirect, teaching for a child to sing:

> The rich man in his castle,
>   The poor man at his gate,
> God made them high or lowly
>   And ordered their estate.

Or:

> There's a friend for little children
>   Above the bright blue sky.

Or again:

> There's a wicked spirit
>   Watching round you still,
> And he tries to tempt you,
>   To all harm and ill.

Doubtless opinions will continue to be divided as to the suitability of this hymn or that, but the important thing is for schools to try to see that the teaching which is done indirectly through the Assembly does not conflict with, but so far as possible, re-inforces, that which is given explicitly in the classroom.

It will be recognised of course, that the influence of hymns and prayers which are used in the Assembly is not always in direct proportion to the extent to which they fall within the range of vocabulary and comprehension of all the children taking part. T. S. Eliot once declared that 'genuine poetry can communicate before it is understood', and much the same holds good of hymns and prayers. Some of the great hymns of praise will carry quite a lot of inner meaning to the younger child even while he does not yet fully comprehend the meaning of every word in every line. One example from among several others would be the hymn which begins:

> Immortal, invisible, God only wise,
> In light inaccessible hid from our eyes,
> Most blessed, most glorious, the ancient of days,
> Almighty, victorious, thy great Name we praise.

And another:

Glorious things of thee are spoken,
Sion, city of our God!
He whose word cannot be broken
Formed thee for his own abode:
On the Rock of Ages founded,
What can shake thy sure repose?
With salvation's walls surrounded,
Thou may'st smile at all thy foes.

So too with some of the prayers which have been used in adult worship down the centuries.

It is customary for readings to be taken mainly from the Bible and while this is right and natural, a certain number could profitably be taken from other sources. The advantages of this arrangement are two: first that by means of it there is avoided a certain monotony in the form of the service, but second and more important, the connection between religion and everyday people and affairs is thereby emphasised. In the Bibliography will be found details of one or two books which provide excellent source-material for the selection of readings of this kind. Details are also there given of some of the books of prayers which are compiled especially with the needs of schools in mind. They include, in addition to prayers of the more usual kind, forms of service and simple Litanies in which the children can join, which enable the head or the teacher taking the Assembly to plan a wide and varied number of services for it.

As most head-teachers look for and receive the co-operation of the Divinity specialist on the school staff in the planning of the Assembly, so they also profit from the advice and assistance of their music teacher. A short musical excerpt, skilfully chosen, and lasting perhaps only two or three minutes, to which the children are encouraged to listen at the beginning of the service and as a real part of it, can do much to create an atmosphere in which the 'things of the spirit' can be approached naturally and positively. It is perhaps worth making the further point that what is here suggested is something much more definite and deliberate than simply providing a musical background for the assembling of the various groups of children. Many musicians indeed feel, with some justification, that the use of music as a background to the shuffling of many feet is a bad thing in itself, and that good music is worthy of conscious attention. What is advocated here is the conscious listening to good music as an essential first stage in the Assembly itself.

The opinion of the musicians on the school staff as to suitable tunes for hymns will also help to ensure that the tune suits the hymn and that hymns are not sung to tunes which in themselves are unsuitable for effective congregational singing by children. Some tunes commonly associated in Church services with certain hymns make for dull and dirgelike singing which can be particularly undesirable in a school Assembly. Others have customarily been used even though musically they contradict, or conflict with, the words of the hymn. In these cases alternative tunes which are musically in keeping with the hymn itself are to be preferred. On all these matters the advice of the musicians on the staff can be of great value.

Where a school has a choir of its own obviously it can be made use of in the Assembly, not only to lead the singing and to encourage the use of a wider selection of hymns, but sometimes to sing a short psalm, or to add a descant to a hymn-tune, or to sing a short anthem on special occasions. Similarly, the existence of a school orchestra offers still further opportunities of enhancing the musical side of the services. It is true that there are certain dangers which can arise from the over-zealous attention to musical matters in connection with the service, but it must be confessed that more school Assemblies suffer from the lack of attention to their musical details than the opposite. In any case, over-meticulous fussing about the music can be avoided if it is borne in mind that the music is here subordinate to a larger aim and not an end in itself.

The school service is usually held in the hall in which a number of other activities take place — meals, physical education, school plays and the like. It follows that children will not easily feel that these surroundings, with their other associations, are particularly conducive to a spirit of religious worship. There is, then, the need to provide some small additions to the furnishings of the hall platform from which the Assembly is normally conducted. It may be possible, for instance, to have a large print of some notable picture dealing with a religious subject, hung at the back of the platform: it can be covered during the rest of the day by a simple curtain. Even if this is not thought desirable, for one reason or another, it should be perfectly feasible to arrange that, for the service, the centre of the platform be occupied, not by the person conducting the service (who can better take up a position to the side) but by a table, perhaps covered with a white linen cloth, on which may stand a plain wooden cross and some flowers.[1] Details of this sort may sound trivial but in the experience of those who have given attention to them, they make a difference to the whole spirit in which the Assembly is conducted, out of all proportion to their intrinsic importance.

In a number of schools the view is taken that children are helped in their worship when the service is occasionally conducted by groups of the children themselves. In some cases a whole class will be given the responsibility for choosing the lections, prayers and hymns for a week and the prayers may include some which have been compiled by the children. Certain members of the class then take it in turn to conduct

---

[1] When this suggestion was made at a Conference of teachers, one member of the audience protested that the provision of a cross would offend against the 1944 Act's insistence that no denominational distinctions must be introduced into the conduct and arrangement of the Assembly. Pressed to explain how, he said that he had Jewish children in mind. In case a similar misunderstanding exists in the minds of others, it is worth pointing out that the denominational distinctions referred to in the Act are those which affect only the Anglican and Free Churches. The Act provides for others by allowing the right of withdrawal. Teachers do not have to attempt the well-nigh impossible task of arranging an Assembly in which children of all denominations and faiths can worship acceptably.

the various parts of the Assembly each morning. The advantages of this arrangement are, it is said, (1) that the arrangement of the service is likely to be such as will more certainly appeal to the children, since it is done by children themselves, and (2) that because for a period the service is actually conducted by the children, a freshness is brought into the services which can sometimes be lacking if they are always taken by the head or members of the staff. While all this is no doubt true, it has to be remembered that there are certain additional hazards which have to be guarded against when groups of children are responsible for the Assembly. It is extremely important that some adult supervision be exercised when the choice of lections, prayers and hymns is being discussed. It is also important to ensure that there should be some rehearsal of the actual conduct of the services, if only to obviate the danger that an error in pronunciation or some other mistake may give rise to the kind of disturbance to which gatherings of young people are prone and which could quickly ruin the whole atmosphere of a service of this kind. Provided these points are watched, however, experience would suggest that the Assembly can take on added value if the children themselves occasionally take over responsibility for the arrangement and conduct of it.

In a chapter dealing with the School Assembly, it would be unrealistic not to face the fact that in gatherings of teachers where religious education is the subject of discussion, exception is more often taken to the compulsory holding of the daily Assembly upon which the Act insists, than to the equally compulsory provision of religious teaching. This is not by any means simply because some teachers are opposed to the school having anything to do with religious education of any kind. More often, it arises from the fact that many teachers feel that unless the Assembly is conducted by adults who are themselves genuine believers, the whole thing becomes hypocritical and that this state of affairs is highly undesirable, above all where the education of the young is concerned.

It is well to recall, at the outset, that from the legal point of view, participation in the religious worship in the school is not compulsory for any teacher. A teacher who so wishes can exercise his right to withdraw from this, as from religious teaching, without detriment to his prospects.

Few would disagree that, from the standpoint of what is ideally desirable, the Assembly should be conducted by individuals who themselves think it important and who can bring life and meaning into the service because they themselves know from their own experience the value of religious worship. Yet, if this principle were strictly followed, it is obvious that some head-teachers and a proportion of their staffs would feel that they ought never to take part in the Assembly at all and this would lead to practical difficulties of a different kind. Conscientious teachers realise that if the head-teacher or a noticeably large proportion of the staff in any school regularly absent themselves from the Assembly, the children will certainly register the fact and draw their own conclusions. To the children, they argue, this will seem a case of advocating, 'Don't do what we do, but do what we say.' Some heads will also take the view that as the Assembly is part of the life of the school in its corporate aspect, the absence from it of members of the staff means a weakening of its corporate activities. Finally, on the important question of promotion, teachers feel that in spite of what the Act says, their chances of being appointed to a headship, especially in a junior school, may well be jeopardised if they are frank about their desire not to have to conduct the Assembly, when they are competing with candidates for the post who are ready to do so.

These problems stem, of course, from the fact that the staffs of our schools, like the children in them, are representative of the community as a whole and so inevitably include people of various shades of religious belief and practice, from the more or less orthodox, to some who would, if pressed, say that they have no definite religious convictions, and perhaps a few who are positively anti-religious. Even if the Act had made no stipulation about the holding of a daily service in all schools, the essential problem whether to have one would still remain: the only difference would be that someone else would have to solve it. The Act solves it for the schools while at the same time preserving the individual's right of conscience. The practical difficulties which arise in the Assembly can be overcome if head-teachers and their staffs are ready, both to adopt a common-sense approach and, even more important, to think first of the educational needs of the children for whom, after all, the Assembly is primarily provided.

On the first point, a reasonable view would be that any head-teacher or member of his staff should feel free to attend the Assembly, and to conduct it, if desired, provided that he is ready to do so reverently and provided also that he is not positively anti-religious. But the successful application of a principle of this kind pre-supposes that teachers should be ready to put the needs of the children before their own personal inclinations. William Temple once made this point in a direct reference to teachers' attitudes to the School Assembly when he declared:

> 'I think teachers are a little liable to ignore the fact that while it is objectionable to force the teachers to conduct prayers against their consciences, it is also objectionable to force the children to omit prayers for the sake of the teachers' consciences.'

The point is well made and is rooted in a sound educational principle. As with the provision of religious teaching, so also with the holding of regular acts of worship in school. It is not normally given to any teacher to know whether or not these daily acts of worship will ultimately turn out to have been important for the development of the children who attend them, any more than it is possible to tell what contribution games, or lessons in art or music will later prove to have made. As an educationist, the teacher certainly has not the right to assume that only what appeals to him, or is thought by him to be important, is always best for the children. Religious worship has evidently been very important for some men and women, and is so still for some today. It is reasonable to assume that for some of the children who pass through any school, it will later prove to have been important as well. In the light of this probability, what matters is that the teacher should strive to make the Assembly as good as it can be so that the worship which it makes possible may make its own contribution to the education, in the deepest sense, of some at least of the children.

CHAPTER 14

RELIGION AND OTHER SUBJECTS

THE title of this book, to say nothing of other considerations, requires that something be said, even in a volume which has been much concerned with the actual teaching of religion, about the connection between religion and the other subjects in the curriculum. Comment is also called for as to the contribution which the teacher who is personally interested in religion but does not teach it, can make to the religious education of children in school.

The emphasis which has been put in earlier chapters on the need for well-informed teaching about religion rooted in sound academic standards, must in no sense be taken to imply that religious education is confined to the Scripture lesson and the worship in Assembly. This would be both a denial of plain fact and a contradiction of the centuries-old Christian concern for education in all its aspects. The facts are that a teacher who believes religion is important will exert a religious influence upon his pupils whatever he teaches, partly through his own character and outlook and partly also in the way he teaches his subject. From the standpoint of the traditional Christian concern with education, the principle has been maintained, from the early centuries of the Christian era up to the present time, that the whole work of education falls within the purview of religion, since education is meant to foster the development of God's creatures in the world which God has created.

It is this last point which tends to get lost sight of nowadays. The Christian humanism which was a strong force in educational thinking and practice in the years immediately

170

following the Reformation and the Renaissance, and for some time after, has in the last hundred years given place to various types of secular humanistic thought and practice. As was said in an earlier chapter, education is now popularly accepted as a thing that is good-in-itself. The development in the young of their various abilities and aptitudes is assumed to be a natural and proper aim of education not needing any re-inforcement from Christian or other religious views of the meaning of human life. It may be argued, if one wishes to do so, that such convictions have their roots in the older Christian attitude to life and its purpose, and to that extent are intrinsically religious. Or it may said that they have nothing directly to do with religion and can be traced back to the egalitarian thinking which issued in the French Revolution. In any case, this kind of debate is somewhat academic and inconclusive. Of much more importance is it to notice that whatever the origins of this secular humanistic approach to educational thought and practice, it tends increasingly to push religion aside and into a position in which it appears at best, as one 'subject' side by side with other (and more important) ones.

This is more noticeable in the higher levels of education than it is at the school stage, because in this country, at any rate, religion is given a more definite place, and more importance, at school level through educational legislation. In the universities, however, it competes to a greater extent on the basis of merits and demand. As we have already noticed, in this sphere it tends to be more neglected than do even the rest of the Humanities— a fairly clear measure of the extent to which it has ceased to exercise more than a fraction of its former influence over education as a whole. Perhaps theological studies themselves are partly to blame for this state of affairs, in that they have become highly specialised during the last seventy-five years or so and at the same time more and more out of touch with other increasingly specialised studies. The gulf between the sciences and theology is more noticeable than most and though sporadic attempts are made to bridge it here and there[1] they do little to bring about a real harmony of view.

But in relation to the study of the Humanities generally, the division becomes more and more apparent. A recent broadcast went to the length of suggesting that modern literature is becoming 'a kind of scripture (and), literary criticism . . . its theology'.[2] History is largely looked upon as a study which is properly approached from a purely secular standpoint, even though at least two distinguished historians have given religion an important place in their thinking and writing.[3] Most recently, philosophy, which of all the Humanities stood for longest in a more or less close relationship with theology, has made a determined effort to free itself from the old associations and to such an extent that at least one Christian philosopher has been moved to attempt a fresh justification of religious ideas and language which is more in keeping with the methods of recent linguistic philosophy.[4]

It was, of course, with this increasing gulf between the religious and the secular in education that Sir Walter Moberly was concerned in his book *The Crisis in the University*.[5] In face of it, he argued that it was necessary that Christian educationists should accept the fact that religion has no privileged position in the universities and that scholars, students and teachers who shared a belief in the importance of religion should work together with the aim of exercising influence on the university as a whole and 'seek to play the rôle of a "creative minority", from which the whole com-

---

[1] E.g., E. L. Mascall, in his Bampton Lectures, published under the title *Christian Theology and Natural Science*, London, 1956, and C. A. Coulson, in his book *Science and Christian Belief*, Oxford, 1955.

[2] Graham Hough: 'The Muse and Her Chains', *Listener* Vol. 67, No. 1727, May 3, 1962, pp. 763–5.

3 Prof. Arnold Toynbee's massive work, *A Study of History*, Oxford, 1933–39, and his *Christianity among the Religions of the World*, 1958, and Prof. Herbert Butterfield in his *Christianity and History*, London, 1949.

4 Prof. I. T. Ramsay in his book *On Religious Language*, London, 1957, and *Freedom and Immortality*, London, 1960.

5 London, 1949.

munity may gradually take colour'.[1] Much the same point has been made by Professor Harbison, the American historian, in an essay which he contributed to the symposium *The Christian Idea of Education*.[2] The issue is also very much in the minds of a group of university teachers in this country who, though working in various fields, are all concerned with the place and influence which religion should have in the universities, and are aware that it is a matter which assumes even greater significance as new universities are coming into existence.[3]

Though we are here mainly concerned with the question of the relation between religion and other subjects in schools, it will be obvious that what is happening both in higher education and in the schools is part and parcel of the same issue. What Sir Walter Moberly suggested as a necessary attitude and aim for religion at the level of university teaching and research holds good of its place in the schools also. The Christian is bound to be concerned with the teaching of all subjects at all levels, however much he must feel a particular concern about explicitly 'religious' teaching. And this is a conviction which stems from precisely the same belief that Christians held when they first founded schools and colleges in the past, namely, that Christianity is concerned with the whole of life and that what children and young people learn about life should be presented in terms of a life which God has given, to be understood and lived for purposes which are in harmony with the mind of God. Professor W. R. Niblett touches on the same point when he says:

> 'A Christian school is not necessarily one in which a considerable proportion of the week is given to worship or divinity, but rather a community having a sense that life is

---

[1] Op. cit., esp. pp. 300–1.

[2] Ed. E. Fuller, New Haven, 1957.

[3] The University Teachers Group. For a recent book which touches on this issue, see *The Expanding University*, Ed. W. R. Niblett, London, 1962.

not a man's to do as he likes with, and aware that all its members older and younger are equally God's children.'[1]

Does this then imply that for the Christian there is something like 'Christian' mathematics, or English, or biology? If by this question is meant that there is a difference between the facts which the Christian and the non-Christian teacher presents to his pupils, or in the scrupulous honesty with which they encourage them to evaluate and assess the facts, the answer is most definitely that there is not. Facts are 'sacred' to the good teacher whether he holds to this or to that view of religion, politics, or anything else. Integrity of thought is no prerogative of the religious teacher but is a quality which all good teachers have in common. In this sense, then, there is no such thing as 'Christian' teaching of any subject — not even of theology itself.[2]

In another sense, however, it is clear that there will be a difference — a difference in the manner in which the facts are related or unrelated to larger and wider issues, and sometimes, a difference in the way they are evaluated. The most obvious examples occur in relation to the teaching of the sciences. The agnostic teacher of biology will feel no obligation to suggest to his pupils that there is anything more to biology than the factual study of plants and animals. The Christian teacher, on the other hand, will make it plain that this is only part of the story, that though man is closely tied to the animals, he is not just an animal, that he possesses abilities and powers which can lift him above them, and the existence of which may not be able to be explained by purely material 'mutations'.[3] The agnostic may be content to

[1] In an Article, *Religious Education and 'Other Subjects'*, in *Religion in Education*, Vol. 27, No. 1, Autumn, 1959.

[2] See Prof. J. Burnaby's Inaugural Lecture delivered in 1953, published as *Education, Religion, Learning and Research*, Camb., n.d.

[3] Not that all biologists, by any means, think that it is yet possible to explain fully the chemical processes which were responsible for the appearance of living creatures. 'It seems to be important that scientists should not pretend to know more than they do. To say, in effect, as some writers have, "Once upon a time a DNA molecule and a protein

suggest that the story of evolution should be understood in and by itself as a purely factual account of a development. The Christian teacher will certainly wish to show that the study of how things 'evolved' does not of itself exclude the notion that the evolution is part of a larger process. Indeed, all Christian teachers of the sciences will probably part company with their agnostic colleagues in wanting to make the point that science represents one kind of approach to the understanding of the universe and that it begins with presuppositions, as does religion.

No doubt, however, it is in the teaching of subjects in which human activities, values and ideals are the focus of attention that the Christian and the non-Christian teacher are bound to traverse more obviously common ground, for in these aspects of study some evaluation of human activities will be made. History is plainly a 'subject' which comes, in part at any rate, into this kind of category and some historians would claim that the study of it, even at school level, itself helps to develop a sense of values. Dr. A. L. Rowse, has called it, among other things 'A science of judgement. It is all the time concerned with human beings and their affairs; so that even at school it elicits judgement of human conduct, for it is an extension of our common-sense experience of it.'[1]

The Christian teacher of history will certainly be concerned to give due weight, among these values, to the religious and spiritual, which have played an important part

---

molecule met and joined together, and later on a cell was formed and this is how it all happened", is a kind of scientific one-upmanship.' (C. Vernon: 'The Origin of Life', *Listener,* Vol. 67, No. 1728. May 10, 1962.)

[1] Op cit. p. 183. My colleague, Mr. W. H. Burston, in an essay on *The Place of History in Education,* argues along somewhat similar lines that 'history is essentially an imaginative study . . . the process of studying it is a process of living in imagination in some past age', which can lead to 'the acquisition of a sense of values between different aspects of life in a community.' University of London, Institute of Education Handbook for History Teachers, London, 1962, p. 11.

in human affairs. He will also presumably have to come to terms with that Biblical view of the ultimate meaning and purpose of history to which reference was made in an earlier chapter, for it affects not only the teaching of Biblical history itself, but the view one takes of history in general. However the teacher understands the 'Divine dimension' in relation to history, the possibility that history can be viewed in this sort of way is an issue which the Christian teacher of history is almost bound to raise in his teaching.

No doubt also, particular events or movements about which his pupils will learn may be presented by a history teacher in a manner which is either more or less sympathetic to religion. The Crusades and the Slave Trade, for example, can either be presented as appalling indictments of the faith of the Christians who took part in them. or did nothing to prevent them, or they can be presented in a way which sets the same stark facts against a background of the morality and general ideas prevailing at the times at which they took place. As the history teacher well knows, European history contains numerous events and movements of a similarly discreditable kind where religion was apparently incapable of lifting men's attitudes and policies above the general level prevailing at those times. Examples abound from as far back as St. Paul's toleration of the institution of slavery, down to the failure of Christianity in recent times to prevent two world wars. Whether a teacher is content merely to expose such apparent inconsistencies, or is concerned also to draw a distinction between religion as ideal and as practice, will doubtless depend in the last resort upon whether he is antagonistic, indifferent, or sympathetic to, religion.[1]

In the teaching of literature, music, painting, and other forms of art, the teacher is concerned, more than is the case with other aspects of teaching, with the communication of

[1] Doubtless the Christian teacher of history needs at the same time to be on his guard against the opposite danger of countenancing ecclesiastical interpretations of history which are sometimes put forward for polemical purposes. On this, see Butterfield: *Christianity and History,* London, 1949, pp. 132–7.

values. For teaching is here aiming, not merely at the acquisition by the pupil of the techniques which are necessary to the development of literary and artistic skills in the use of words, a pencil or a paint-brush, or the voice or a musical instrument, but also at enriching experience and developing critical judgment.[1] In relation to literature, this kind of aim will involve also the consideration of human character, behaviour, motives, ideals and this in turn may exert an influence upon the outlook and perhaps the behaviour of the pupils themselves.

Doubtless all teachers of literature and the arts would accept without question that among their responsibilities is that of trying to help their pupils to learn to distinguish between 'good' and 'bad' literature and art. They would probably also agree that it is certainly not part of their task to seek to identify 'good' with any sectional point of view, whether of a religious, or any other, variety. In this sense again, therefore, there can be no such thing as a 'Christian' selection of suitable literature[2], or paintings or music for study in school, or a 'Christian' treatment of what is selected. The Christian teacher of literature or the arts will be as concerned as his agnostic colleague to make his selection and his presentation of material on the basis of artistic merit, and to make it as representative as is compatible with the ability of, and stage of development reached by, the particular group of pupils he is teaching. Yet no teacher can escape from the larger task of helping young people to relate

[1] 'What we are after through the study of literature is bringing to consciousness in our pupils what is involved in being human. One of the prime purposes is to enlarge insight into human motive; to increase the range and profundity of understanding of human character; gradually to improve ability to judge the depth and scope of the experiences a boy or girl gets from reading and listening to literature.'

'The main direction of English teaching should be from experiencing, through comprehension, to evaluation.' Niblett: *Christian Education in a Secular Society*, Oxf. 1960, pp. 55–6.

[2] And certainly not a selection limited to 'Christian' writers, even though, as was suggested in an earlier chapter, a good deal of literature cannot be fully appreciated without some understanding of Christianity.

to life as he and others understand it, the experiences which thus come to light, and the ideas and values implicit in them, and at this point the difference between the outlook of the teacher who is sympathetic to religion and the one who is not, will most obviously manifest itself.

Like his colleague teaching history, so the teacher of literature or the arts who values religion, will tend to relate the experiences and values of which his pupils become aware through his teaching, to issues of a larger kind which his a-religious colleague will probably not wish to raise to anything like the same extent. In his hands the widening and deepening experience which can come through literature and the arts will be seen against a background of man's full potentialities. There is a frame of reference, as it were, which, though it will not be allowed to obtrude into the teaching or distort it, will lead his pupils to consider man in his spiritual, as well as his physical, emotional and intellectual aspects; to see him as a free and responsible being, not merely as a creature shackled to his own or an evolutionary past; to watch him living with a sense of purpose and not simply as a slave of impulse or circumstance.

It will be observed then, that if the point of view adopted in this chapter is sound, the same essential characteristic tends to distinguish the work of the religious teacher of 'other subjects', whatever they may be, from that of his colleagues who take a secular point of view in their teaching. It may be described, perhaps, as breadth of view. For him, the insights which are to be gained from the study of a particular subject are more obviously partial, fragments of a larger whole which has to be kept in mind. Man is more than biology, or chemistry, or psychology can reveal about him; human history can be but partially comprehended as a process beginning and ending with itself; science is but one 'way of knowing'; literature and the arts reveal man as a many-sided, even a contradictory, and not a simple being, and so on. This, or something like it, will always be the unspoken but insistent emphasis which the religiously minded teacher will bring to his teaching in many and various spheres. His pupils will find that 'their feet have been set in a large room' and that their eyes have been opened to the 'mystery' of life.

'He that knows the secrets of nature with Albertus Magnus, or the motions of the heavens with Galileo, or the cosmography of the moon with Hevelius, or the body of man with Galen, or the nature of diseases with Hippocrates, or the harmonies in melody with Orpheus, or of poetry with Homer, or of grammar with Lily, or of whatever else with the greatest artist; he is nothing if he knows them merely for talk or idle speculation, or transient and external use. But he that knows them for value, and knows them as his own, shall profit infinitely.'[1]

[1] Thomas Traherne *Centuries of Meditations*.

BIBLIOGRAPHY

Besides the books already referred to in the footnotes, the following will be found useful. It should be emphasised that the list represents a selection from those which are available.

PRINCIPLES AND METHODS OF TEACHING

Avery, M., *Teaching Scripture* (Relig. Ed. Press).

Avery, M., *Religious Education in the Secondary Modern School* (Relig. Ed. Press).

Doidge & Thomson, *Film Strip Do's and Don'ts* (Relig. Ed. Press).

Gullan, M., *Choral Speaking* (Methuen).

Jones, C. M., *The Methods of Christian Education* (Student Christian Movement Press).

Murray, A. V., *Teaching the Bible, especially in Secondary Schools* (C.U.P.).

Sims-Williams, M., *Religion through Drama* (S.C.M.).

Watts, A., *No New Thing* (S.P.C.K.).

Youngman, B. R., *Teaching Religious Knowledge* (U.L.P.).

VERSIONS OF THE BIBLE AND SHORTENED VERSIONS

The Bible in the Authorised Version (with line maps and illustrations by John Stirling), (Brit. & For. Bible Socy.).

The American Revised Standard Version of the Holy Bible (Nelson).

The New English Bible, New Testament (O. and C.U.P.).

The New Testament in Modern English, Trans. by J. B. Phillips (School Ed.) Bles.

The Shorter Oxford Bible (School Ed.) (O.U.P.).

A Beginner's Bible, M. Fanchiotti and N. Micklem (O.U.P.).

TEXT BOOKS FOR USE IN THE SECONDARY SCHOOL

(1st – 3rd Years)

Braley, E. F., *The Life and Teaching of Jesus* (Books 1, 2 and 3), (Nelson).

Braley, E. F., *The Acts of the Apostles* (Books 1 and 2), (Nelson).

Sands, P. C., *Men of God* (S.P.C.K.).

Thompson, R. W., *English Christianity Handbooks*:

Vol. 1 *How Christianity came to England.*
Vol. 2 *How Christianity grew in England.*
Vol. 3 *How Christianity spread in England.*
Vol. 4 *How the English Bible Grew* (R.E.P.).

Walker, V., *A First Church History* (S.C.M.).
Youngman, B. R., *Background to the Bible*:

Vol. 1 *Patriarchs, Judges and Kings.*
Vol. 2 *Prophets and Rulers.*
Vol. 3 *The Palestine of Jesus.*
Vol. 4 *The Spreading of the Gospel* (Hulton Ed. Pubns.)

(4th – 5th Years)

Bull, N. J., *Jesus and His Teaching* (R.E.P.)
Firth, C. B. (ed.), *The Bible and the Christian Faith*:

Vol. 1 *Christ in the Gospels.*
Vol. 2 *Christ in the Early Church.*
Vol. 3 *A People of Hope.*
Vol. 4 *Poets, Wise Men and Seers.*
Vol. 5 *Christian Conduct.*
Vol. 6 *From Bible to Creed* (Ginn).

Fleming, E., *From Solomon to Herod* (S.C.M.)
Foster, J., *Beginning from Jerusalem* (Lutterworth)
Foster, J., *After the Apostles* (S.C.M.)
Heaton, E., *The Old Testament Prophets* (Pelican)
Payne, E. A., *The Growth of the World Church* (Edin. Hse. Press)
Robinson, W., *The Shattered Cross*: the Many Churches and the One
    Church (Berean Press)
Smart, W. J., *Walking with God*: Lives of Twelve great Christians of
    modern times (Hodder & Stoughton)
Snaith, N. H., *The Jews from Cyrus to Herod* (R.E.P.)
Stedman, A. R., *The Beginnings of the Christian Church* (Bell)
Walton, R. C. (ed.), *Modern Bible Textbooks*:

Battle for a City — First Isaiah.
The Fall of a City — Book of Jeremiah.
Two Refugees — Ezekiel and Second-Isaiah.
A Gospel for Martyrs — St. Mark's Gospel.
The King's Story — St. Matthew's Gospel.
A Doctor's Life of Jesus — St. Luke's Gospel (S.C.M.)

(G.C.E.)

Guy, H. A., *The Life of Christ* (Macmillan)
Guy, H. A., *A Critical Introduction to the Gospels* (Macmillan)
Guy, H. A., *The Synoptic Gospels* (Macmillan)
Guy, H. A., *The Acts of the Apostles* (Macmillan)
Kibblewhite, K. N. (ed.), *The London Divinity Series*:

Vol. 1 *Israel to the time of Solomon.*
Vol. 2 *From Solomon to the Captivity.*

Vol. 3   *From the Exile to New Testament Times.*
Vol. 4   *The Life and Teaching of Jesus Christ.*
Vol. 5   *The Acts of the Apostles and the Letters of St. Paul.*
Vol. 6   *The Johannine Writings and Other Epistles* (James
         Clarke)

Robinson, H. W., *The History of Israel* (Duckworth)
Robinson, H. W., *Religious Ideas of the Old Testament.* (Duckworth)

PALESTINIAN LIFE AND CUSTOMS

Bouquet, A. C., *Everyday Life in New Testament Times* (Batsford)
Entwistle, M., *The Bible Guide Book* (S.C.M.)
Hastings, J. (ed.), *Dictionary of the Bible* (T. and T. Clark)
Heaton, E., *Everyday Life in Old Testament Times* (Batsford)
Hilliard, F. H., *Behold the Land.* A Pictorial Atlas of the Bible (G. Philip)
Kohler, L., *Hebrew Man.*
Wiseman, D. J., *Illustrations from Biblical Archæology* (Tyndale Press)
Wright, G. E., *Biblical Archæology* (Duckworth)

ATLASES AND WALL MAPS

Grollenberg, L. H., *Atlas of the Bible* (Nelson)
Hilliard, F. H., *Behold the Land.* A Pictorial Atlas of the Bible (G. Philip)
New Scripture Atlas (G. Philip)
Westminster Smaller Atlas (S.C.M.)
Wall Atlas of Bible Lands (Series of 8) (G. Philip)
Wall Maps (from Westminster Historical Atlas to the Bible) (Series of 6)
         (S.C.M.)
Mapograph Contours for Religious Instruction (Series of 7) (Mapograph
         Co. Ltd.)

SCHOOL WORSHIP

(General)

Ferguson, J. M. M., *The School Assembly* (R.E.P.)
Payne, E. O., *Music in the School Assembly* (R.E.P.)
Williams, J. G., *Worship and the Modern Child* (S.P.C.K.)
Williams, J. G., *Leading School Worship* (S.P.C.K.)

(Service Books, Prayers and Readings)

Blackburn, E. A., *A Treasury of the Kingdom* (O.U.P.)
Bouquet, A. C., *A Lectionary of Christian Prose* (Longmans)
Dent and Martin, *Worship in the Junior School* (S.P.C.K.)
Martin, H. (ed.), *A Book of Prayers for Schools* (S.C.M.)
Prescott, D. M. (ed.), *Infant Teachers' Assembly Book* (Blandford Press)
Prescott, D. M. (ed.), *Junior Teachers' Assembly Book* (Blandford Press)
Shambrook, R. J., *Daily Worship* (U.L.P.)

         Oxford Book of School Worship (Part 1, Infants; Part 2,
         Junior and Senior) (S.P.C.K.)

The Daily Service (O.U.P.)
Two-minute Bible Readings (S.C.M.)

(Hymn Books)

B.B.C. Hymn Book (O.U.P.)
English School Hymn Book (U.L.P.)
Songs of Praise (O.U.P.)

JOURNALS FOR THE TEACHER

Learning for Living (S.C.M.)
The Expository Times (T. and T. Clark)
Theology (S.P.C.K.)
View-Review (S.P.C.K.)
Journal of Theological Studies (O.U.P.)
Journal of Ecclesiastical History (Nelson)

FILMSTRIPS

(Junior or Secondary)

Dwellers in Bible Lands (Picture Post, Education Dept., Hulton Press Ltd. London, E.C.4.)
Two Thousand Years Ago Series (Religious Films, 6 Eaton Gate, London, S.W.1):

> *The Home.*
> *The Day's Work.*
> *The School.*
> *The Travellers.*
> *Synagogue and Passover.*

(Secondary)

Bible:

> *Background to the Old Testament,* 1–4 (Picture Post)
> *Background of St. Paul,* 1–2 (Picture Post)
> *Discoveries at Ur* (Carwal Ltd., 85 Manor Road, Wallington, Surrey)
> *The Story of our Bible* (Common Ground, 44 Fulham Road, London, S.W.3.)
> *The Ancient World, Life in Ancient Palestine* (Common Ground, 44 Fulham Road, London, S.W.3.)

History of the Church:

> *The Spread of Christianity Series* (Common Ground, 44 Fulham Road, London, S.W.3.):
> *The Winning of the Roman Empire.*
> *The Upbuilding of Christendom.*
> *Along New Routes.*
> *World Wide.*
> *The Great Advance.*

The Universal Church.
Christianity in Africa.

Biography (Common Ground, 44 Fulham Road, London, S.W.3.):

Albert Schweitzer.
David Livingstone.
Dr. Barnardo.
John Wesley.
Wilfred Grenfell.

World Religions:

Introduction to World Religions.
Islam (Common Ground.)
Judaism — A Way of Life (Carwal Ltd.)
The Synagogue (Hulton Edl. Publns.)
Life Filmstrips (in colour) (Life Filmstrips, 9 Rockefeller Plaza, N. York 20, N. York.):

Part 1 *Hinduism.*
Part 2 *Buddhism.*
Part 3 *Confucianism and Taoism.*
Part 4 *Islam.*

FILMS

Bible:

Jordan Valley — A Study of Palestine and its people, illustrating many of the ideas and sayings of the Bible. (Black & White)
Two Thousand Years Ago Series. (Same Titles as for Filmstrips) (Black and White)

History of the Church:

David Livingstone (Black and White)
The Great Heart — Story of Father Damien (Black and White)

All these on hire from: Educational Foundation for Visual Aids, Bracklands House, Weybridge, Surrey.

Gospel of Stone — Stone carvings in French churches and Cathedrals. (Black and White)

Available from: Central Film Library, Government Building, Bromyard Avenue, London, W.3.

INDEX